INVESTIGATING
MICROECONOMICS

To my friend
Lou Tokle

INVESTIGATING MICROECONOMICS

Jim Eggert

WILLIAM KAUFMANN, INC. LOS ALTOS, CALIFORNIA

Graphics by Karen Markotic
Cover illustration suggested by Tom Cambron
Book design and composition by: Information Design, Inc.,
                                 Salt Lake City, Utah

Library of Congress Cataloging in Publication Data

Eggert, Jim, 1943-
     Investigating microeconomics.

     Includes bibliographical references and index.
     1. Microeconomics. I. Title.
HB171.5.E464   338.5   79-16480
ISBN 0-913232-62-9
ISBN 0-913232-61-0 pbk.

Contents

PREFACE

While he was living in Boston and working on the second edition of *Leaves of Grass,* the great American poet Walt Whitman wrote his brother Jeff a letter. It was an interesting letter, which not only included information about his new book, but also a strong statement concerning the prices of coffee and beefsteak:

> Oh, the awful expense I have been under here, Jeff, living the way I have, hiring a room, and eating at restaurants—7 cents for a cup of coffee, and 19 cts for a beefsteak—*and me so fond of coffee and beefsteak.**

It is comforting to me as an economist to see that the famous author of *Leaves of Grass* was also concerned (like all the rest of us) with mundane things like the price of coffee and the general economic impact of creature comforts. In fact, it's quite possible that Walt Whitman, with his vast curiosity about almost everything, might also have been interested in the *origin* of prices and of supply and demand, now commonly called microeconomics. It is these subjects that we will examine in this book.

Unfortunately for modern students of economics, "microecon" has not been regarded as a very friendly subject. It is frequently approached with fear and endured with much suffering. I am not quite sure why microeconomics has been disliked, for it *can* be a fascinating subject.

---

*Walt Whitman, *The Correspondence, Vol. 1,* (E.H. Miller, Ed.), New York University Press, 1961, p. 53.

Perhaps one reason is that this subject seems too abstract. In addition, I have noticed that a number of books develop the ideas of microeconomics in a piece-by-piece approach which can make it difficult to see the entire subject as a whole.

In this book, our major emphasis will be on *continuity*. We begin our journey through microeconomics with elementary assumptions of consumer and producer behavior; then we move along the economic terrain to develop a simple model of a supply-demand competitive market. In the second half of the book, we will move into territory that is more realistic and, in a sense, more familiar, as we discuss actual market structures and the varieties and types of American industries.

In the interest of continuity, I have left out some important topics that may be covered in traditional texts. Therefore, this book should *not* be considered a comprehensive microeconomic textbook. But these omissions are offset by looking into more advanced topics which can be more easily understood because of our different approach.

I assume that readers will have had some introductory economic background. What specifically? At a minimum, they should have some knowledge of simple supply and demand analysis as well as an understanding of demand elasticity—topics covered in Chapter 3 of my earlier introductory book, *What Is Economics?* *

My fondest hope is that *Investigating Microeconomics* will help you *connect* things together—that you will get a feeling for the pulse of microeconomics as our analysis moves from pure theory to more real-life situations.

I would like to take a moment to thank a few of the many individuals who have helped me with this project. First and foremost were my microeconomics professors James Dana and the late Charles Ferguson. I would like to also thank my father, Bob Eggert, my wife Patricia, and the numerous readers of the original manuscript including Lou Tokle, Clyde Smith, Dayle Mandelson

*What Is Economics? by Jim Eggert. © 1977 by William Kaufmann, Inc. Los Altos, California 94022

and Ron Gunderson. And finally my warm thanks to my own students who, over the years, have helped me out in more ways than they could possibly realize.

Jim Eggert
University of Wisconsin, Stout
Menomonie, Wisconsin.

Chapter 1

What Is Microeconomics?

Design. I like to think of the economic process as one of design. It is at least a reasonable starting point for our discussion of microeconomics. Microeconomics looks at how the bits and pieces of our economy—you, and I, and the grocer down the street and even the large corporation—how we all design our lives or our organizations to meet certain economic objectives. For some, microeconomics is like a game—a game that has certain rules, constraints and ultimate objectives.

Consumers, for example, are constrained by having only a certain amount of income. On the other hand, businesses must work within the confines of their production costs, their competition, and their demand. Both must obey the rules of the market place.

But what about the goals or objectives of our players? In some social sciences such as psychology or sociology, the objectives are not always clearly defined. In microeconomics, the goal we study is relatively uncomplicated—the goal of *maximization*.

Let us begin with the assumption that when we (as consumers, businesses, workers, or whatever) put on our "economic hats," we attempt to maximize economic goals. Specifically, we'll assume

a. that the consumer will attempt to get the largest amount of utility (satisfaction) from his limited income,
b. that the worker will attempt to maximize income while maintaining or enlarging the amount of leisure time,
c. and that business will attempt to maximize profits within the constraints of costs, demand, and competition.

Economists have been severely critized at times for making and promoting the assumption of "economic-man as maximizer." And perhaps there is some justification. The word, "maximization," itself carries with it a connotation of operating with a kind of brutal efficiency while pursuing profits or enlarging one's income base. Indeed, it has often been alleged that many of our social and economic ills derive from this maximization principle, including worker exploitation, environmental pollution, wars, the disappearance of craftsmanship and of joy in working, and even the destruction of relationships between people. There is probably some truth to these allegations.

In addition, we are presently witnessing attempts in modern societies to develop some alternatives to income maximization in an effort to promote greater worker satisfaction and harmony within our economic environment. We may read about new experiments along this line almost every week. I am intrigued, for example, by a little magazine called *Briarpatch Review – a Journal of Right Livelihood & Simple Living* that has suggested alternatives to profit maximization in small businesses:

> If you take "making a lot of money" off the list of reasons for being in business you can pretty easily replace it with "fun," since you then have time to enjoy yourself by interacting with others.*

Or there is that provocative book *Small is Beautiful* (with its curious subtitle; *Economics as if People Mattered*) in which the author, E. F. Schumacher, describes a number of reasons why people should work, above and beyond the income maximization reason. The purposes of work, Schumacher explains in his chapter "Buddhist Economics," are

> . . . to give a man a chance to utilize and develop his faculties; to enable him to overcome his ego-centeredness by joining with other people in a common task; and to bring forth the goods and services needed for a becoming existence.
> . . . To organize work in such a manner that it becomes meaningless, boring, stultifying, or nerveracking for the worker would be little short of criminal; it would indicate a greater concern with goods than with people...**

---

*Briarpatch Review, "Fun in Business" by Kristen Anundsen and Michael Phillips, Spring, 1977, p. 30.

**Small Is Beautiful, by E.F. Schumacher, © 1973, Harper and Row, pp. 54-55.

Of course, such a view of "making work meaningful" is not exactly a new one. As Schumacher points out, these traditions can be traced back in various sources, including Buddhist philosophy and, more recently, the writings of Thoreau, Tolstoi, and Gandhi.

Microeconomics can sometimes contribute to the creation of a general hostility toward economics because of a tendency to see human beings and organizations in purely *quantitative terms* —that is, the more the quantity of objective x (profits, income, utility, etc.), the better. Again, many economists would agree that there is some truth to this criticism as well.

But on the other hand, I do not think that these are entirely fair criticisms of what we are attempting to do in our very limited world of microeconomics. Most economists *do* realize that monetary maximization is really only part of our total existence. Any business or individual who becomes totally obsessed with narrow economic goals would indeed become a kind of monster and would need to be restrained by government regulations as well as by his fellow beings. Yet persons or businesses who *totally disregard* these economic objectives will undoubtedly find their survival threatened. In this sense, most individuals and businesses *tend toward* maximization goals; that is, our theories of microeconomics frequently *do* reflect the way "the bits and pieces of our economic system behave." To the extent that our observations adhere to reality, they are useful in helping us to understand both ourselves and our organizations.

Finally, I think we are justified in our approach if we look at this maximization process as *symbolic*. This gets us back to the beginning statement of this chapter where we implied that the microeconomic process was a process of design; that is, a life or an organization is designed within the constraints of our limited resources. Maximizing dollars under resource constraints is thus symbolic of *any* process that involves finite resources and freedom of choice. Resources may vary considerably between individuals or groups. In addition, our goals may be as diverse as getting good grades, finding time to write a novel, starting a new business, successfully raising a family, or even combining a number of such goals. If we look at microeconomics in this light, we may well discover some important insights into basic human behavior.

Much of our work in microeconomics will involve the use of graphs. I hope you will become a "Sherlock Holmes" of graphwork. For example, you should eventually be able to glance at a certain kind of graph and say, "Yes, this one represents the behavior of a monopolist who does not seem to be making any profit," or "This graph portrays a consumer who enjoys hamburgers over milkshakes," or "This graph shows us that when this family's income increases by 10%, it will *reduce* its buying of x product by 5%," and so on.

Undoubtedly, you have already come across some graphs in your school work, especially in any earlier courses in economics. One of the most common in an introductory course is the so-called "Keynesian model of aggregate supply and demand," which looks like the one shown in Figure 1-1.

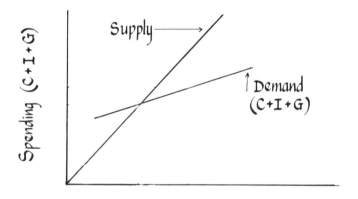

Total Income = GNP = Total Output

fig 1-1

This graph in Figure 1-1 is representative of the subject of *macroeconomics*. "Macro" has always been a more popular topic than "micro" economics mainly because macro deals with those economic issues that we read and hear about all the time — unemployment, inflation, gross national product, and economic growth. On the other hand, most readers have probably had at least some experience using a simple supply and demand graph such as the one shown in Figure 1-2.

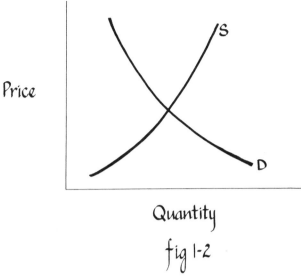

Quantity

fig 1-2

The supply-demand market is representative of our *micro-economic* world. This raises the obvious question as to how we might be able to relate the familiar world of macroeconomics and gross national product to that of microeconomics with its concentration on single markets. The best method of connecting them, I believe, is shown in the "circular-flow" diagram in Figure 1-3.

Notice in Figure 1-3 that households and businesses relate to each other through *resource markets* and *goods and services markets*. It is a good illustration of why we call our economic system a "market economy." At the top of the circular flow diagram are the markets—i.e. supply and demand situations—for land, labor, and capital, our major economic resources. On the bottom are the markets for goods and services; i.e. the supply and demand situations for things like corn, auto repair, and motorcycles. As these markets churn out quantities of all our goods and services through the interactions of businesses and consumers, we have the "piece-by-piece" make-up of the overall gross national product (GNP). GNP is nothing more than the sum total of the productive results of the goods and services markets.

Those who study the major production flows (macro-economics) are mainly interested in the health of the larger system and spend much of their time devising policies which might move the economy closer to the goals of stable prices, economic growth, and full-employment.

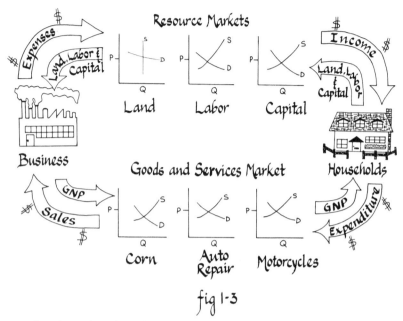

fig 1-3

On the other hand, those who study *microeconomics* spend most of their time analyzing the origin, the make-up, and ultimately the efficiency of *individual resource* or *product markets*. In microeconomics, therefore, we will spend quite a bit of time analyzing where a supply curve comes from or why a demand curve has its unique shape.

In one's earliest study of economics, for example, one learns that an individual's demand curve for a product, (say, hamburgers) is downward sloping, i.e., the curve is "telling us" that as we reduce the price of hamburgers, that particular individual will want more hamburgers. This may indeed be a logical assumption. But so far, we have not actually *proven* that this must always be the case. Establishing such a proof, in fact, is one of our jobs as microeconomists.

Microeconomics invites other questions as well. For example, why does your demand curve for hamburgers look different from mine? Why are some people more sensitive to a price change than others? There are, we find, many subtleties *in back of* that simple looking demand curve, subtleties that challenge us to look deeper and deeper into an individual's economic behavior.

We must therefore engage in a certain amount of economic and psychological snooping if we wish to really understand the origin of demand. We will have to take a close look at the consumer's income, and preferences, as well as the prices of related goods before we will see what lies in back of "Joe Smith's" demand for hamburgers or any other product. And of course, once we understand Joe Smith's demand, we will be able to do the same thing for you or me, or for anyone else. This is what "micro" is all about.

Microeconomics also looks at the supply curve as well. And we cannot be completely satisfied to say, "It's logical that if corn prices go up, Farmer Brown will want to supply more corn." No, we must now dig a little deeper. For example, to fully understand Farmer Brown's supply curve for corn, we must know how the demand situation looks for corn, we must carefully examine Farmer Brown's costs of production, and we will have to set up some procedures so that Brown will know how to maximize his profits at different prices of corn. Indeed, as you see, it can get pretty involved!

But it will be worth it in the end. By the middle of this book we will have built our first competitive market model, and by Chapter 10, we will have explored the supply models, such as monopoly and oligopoly, and will have seen how they relate to each other and to the overall economic system.

Chapter 2

Background to Demand

Consider the source of our economic behavior. What exactly is it? What is the origin of our motivation to engage in economic activity? The answer is, of course, *consumption* —to use goods and services—first, to survive, and beyond that, to enjoy a standard of living commensurate with both our expectations and our dreams. For some individuals, a small amount of consumption will do, but most of us want to have *more*, more of the good things our resources and our economic system can provide.

From this basic assumption of human behavior, we can infer that any amount of consumption brings with it a certain amount of satisfaction—or as economists say, *utility*. Utility is obviously a difficult thing to measure precisely. It's also difficult to make comparisons of utility between people. Your utility, your satisfaction, for example, from the consumption of an automobile or a banana is probably going to be different from mine—or from anybody else's. And there might well be some surprises if we actually could measure utility between people. Depriving you of your fourth Cadillac might result in a greater loss of satisfaction to you than my utility loss if someone took away my one Ford. Even though you have 4 Cadillacs, the loss of one might send you into depression because all your neighbors have 5. Thus, it's very difficult to make any generalizations about one person's utility versus another person's utility.

But we can still say a few useful things about utility as long as we confine our discussion to a single individual. For example, Mary Smith might tell us that she *seems* to be getting about 5 units of utility from eating one hamburger and around 2 units from consuming a banana. Is it possible to check out Mary's intuition?

One way to determine if she is accurate about her utility estimates would be to give her exactly 70 cents and tell her that she is allowed to buy fractions of hamburgers or bananas. Now if we price a full hamburger at 50 cents and a banana at 20 cents and we then observe that Mary spends her 70 cents for exactly one hamburger and one banana, we could then assume that her rough utility ratio of 5 to 2 is correct.

Economists love to dream up ways in which economic relationships (such as utility comparisons) might be quantified—that is, assigned numbers so that numerical relationships can be compared. You are encouraged to dream up your own schemes. You might also try making some utility comparisons for products you frequently consume.

Another interesting observation we can make concerns the consumption of just a single product. Let's return for a minute to our example of your 4 Cadillacs. Even though we might not know exactly how much utility your fourth Cadillac gives you (compared to how much my Ford gives me), we can say with some assurance that you received *more* utility from your *first* Cadillac compared to the fourth. Or, to take a more realistic example, Mary's third hamburger will give her less satisfaction than her second, and her second less than her first. As mentioned earlier, there is no reason why we cannot attach rough utility values to each of these hamburgers. Since I know more about my own utility levels than yours or Mary Smith's, I will make up an example using my own utility preferences. Let's say that after considerable thought and experimentation, I come up with the following utility "schedule":

HAMBURGERS	MARGINAL UTILITY (MUh)
1	7
2	3
3	1
4	0

What this chart is telling us is that the first hamburger I consume will give me 7 units of utility. The next hamburger will give me only 3 added units, and by the time I eat my third my additional utility is only 1 unit. Economists call this "additional utility" (which is assigned to the consumption of a certain unit) *marginal utility* (MU). Obviously I'm starting to get pretty full after 2 hamburgers and after my third hamburger, I am completely full since hamburger #4 is giving me no marginal utility whatsoever. If somebody gave me that fourth hamburger free, I'd leave it on my plate.

Can we make any generalization about this utility pattern? Apparently, the more one consumes of a given product, the less the marginal utility. Indeed, this principle would probably be true no matter who we were talking about and would also be true concerning any particular product that we wished to look at. This pattern is, in fact, such a universal principle that economists have named it *the law of diminishing marginal utility*. It's an economic law that is almost as famous as the familiar law of diminishing returns.

Diminishing marginal utility is worth remembering if you happen to be on a diet since that tenth spoonful of ice-cream (or the fourth cookie) will undoubtedly give you less satisfaction than the first. It may also help explain why marriages sometimes go sour, or once "exciting" jobs eventually become boring. You can surely apply this principle to many of your own experiences.

Sometimes it's helpful to visualize these economic relationships such as the law of diminishing marginal utility on a graph. Using the marginal utility data given above, I am able to graph my diminishing MU curve as in Figure 2-1.

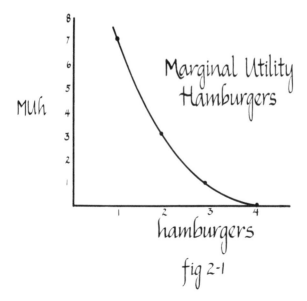

fig 2-1

Keep in mind that the above graph is only *my* marginal utility curve for hamburgers. Your curve, or someone else's, would look somewhat different. You might spend a moment sketching different possibilities—such as the MU curve for a "Whimpy" who can lovingly eat a dozen hamburgers before he gets full. Or what about someone who is more or less "indifferent" to hamburgers? What about your curve; what would it look like?

Now that we understand the principle of diminishing marginal utility, we are prepared to make some interesting observations concerning how a consumer might behave given a *choice* between two products. In other words, how does our theory help discover how I might maximize my satisfactions given a choice of products and a limited income? Maximizing one's satisfaction is the fundamental *economic problem* facing each and every consumer.

To see how I might solve a simple economic problem, let's return to my old hamburger example but now add a new product—say, milkshakes—so that I will be faced with a situation of *choice*. Let's assume that my milkshake marginal utility schedule looks something like this:

MILKSHAKES	MARGINAL UTILITY (MUm)
1	12
2	3
3	½

To be realistic, we should also add an *income constraint*. Let's say that I am given $4 per day. I also find out that the price of a milkshake is $1 and the price of a hamburger is also $1. With all this information, how do I go about "maximizing" my *total utility*, i.e. how do I spend my limited income so that I might enjoy the highest possible level of total satisfaction?

The best method of maximizing my utility would be for me to use what economists call the *marginal decision approach*. Marginal decision making involves making a separate decision for each separate dollar at my disposal; thus, I would take my first dollar and ask the question: "Where will this dollar give me the greatest utility?"

If you compare our chart for milkshakes with that for hamburgers, you can easily see that I should spend my first dollar on milkshake #1, for that first milkshake will give me 12 units of utility while that same dollar would have only given me 7 units of utility had I spent it on hamburger #1.

My marginal decision making approach would then lead me to my next question: How can I best spend my second dollar? Then, how can I best spend my third dollar, and after that, my fourth dollar. A summary of my marginal decisions can be seen in the comparative chart below:

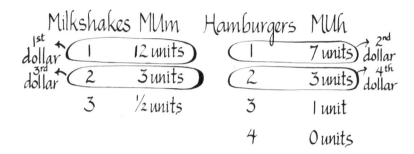

Thus, my second dollar would be spent on a hamburger while the third dollar would be a toss-up since both products would give me the same marginal utility (3 units) per dollar. (In the chart above, I chose a milkshake for my third dollar.) The last dollar spent would, in a sense, "balance things up" so that when all the income had been spent, the marginal utility per dollar's worth of each product (i.e. 3 units/$1) would be equal. If you could obtain more utility from spending your last dollar on another product (french-fries, for example), you would obviously want to spend that dollar on that third product.

Now if we all had a "perfect" world where we knew precisely the marginal utilities of each and every product we consumed, where we could spend our money exactly as we wished—even for a fraction of a hamburger or milkshake, or a quarter of a bag of french-fries—we would then attain the highest possible state of satisfaction if we could "finish up our spending" (i.e. after *all* our dollars were spent) so that the marginal utility per dollar's worth (i.e. the marginal utility divided by the product price—mu/p) of product A would be equal to that of B which would equal that of C . . . and so forth. More generally speaking, the consumer has "solved" his maximization problem when he has spent his limited income so that:

$$\frac{MU_A}{P_A} = \frac{MU_B}{P_B} = \frac{MU_C}{P_C} = \frac{MU_D}{P_D}$$

A = Hamburgers
B = Milkshakes
C = French Fries
D = Other things

In other words, when the above ratios are equal, we can be confident that this particular consumer has spent his limited income to gain the maximum amount of utility.

So far, so good. But there are still people who are greatly bothered by the very inexact science of trying to measure utility by precise numbers as we tried to do in our preceeding example. Is there, in fact, any way that we can discuss the problem of consumer efficiency without having to give actual utility values? Fortunately, the answer to this question is "yes." It's called "the indifference curve system." Let's take a look.

Indifference Curves—

First, some additional background. As we hinted earlier, economists all have a little bit of "the psychologist" in them as well as a little of "the newspaper reporter." Thus, microeconomists could conceivably be running around with pencils and pads asking people different questions relating to their incomes, their consumption habits, their work preferences, their values, and so on. Fair game questions might be something like, "If everything else were equal (that is, nothing changes except those things we want to change), how much more housing . . . or recreation . . . or potatoes would you buy if your income went up by 25%?" "If the price of coffee doubles, how much more tea would you buy?" These kinds of questions can sometimes bring in very interesting answers— answers that give the researcher insight into how consumers will behave under different economic conditions. And eventually our economist-psychologist-reporter might be able to discover some generalized principles (such as the law of diminishing marginal utility) which may become the basis of economic theory. The *indifference curve system* is one of those areas where we can begin by asking some simple questions and can eventually work out some extremely interesting generalizations and conclusions. Let's take an example.

Pretend that you are the economic researcher. You ask me the following questions: "If I gave you 1 milkshake and 3 hamburgers, you would derive a certain amount of utility from that combination, right?"

I answer, "OK," and you then go on: "Let's call that amount of utility *your total utility level* Y. Now if I reduce the number of hamburgers to 2, how many additional milkshakes would you need to keep yourself at total utility level Y?"

Suppose I answer you by saying; "I will need an extra ¼ milkshake to make up for the lost hamburger. That is, I will be totally *indifferent* about consuming either 3 hamburgers and 1 milkshake or a combination of 2 hamburgers and 1¼ milkshakes."

As a final question, you might ask me how many milkshakes I would need if I consumed only 1 hamburger yet wished to stay at total utility level Y. Let's say that I would need 2 full shakes to be indifferent to the other combinations. Below are the results of your research:

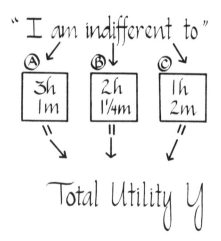

In other words, at the combinations in A or B or C, I would be equally well off. That is, I would be "indifferent" as to consuming at any of these points, since my *total utility* would stay the same in each case.

Is it possible to graph these "points" of indifference? No problem, if we design our indifference curve graph with hamburg-

ers on one scale and milkshakes on the other. Figure 2-2 shows
how this can be done.

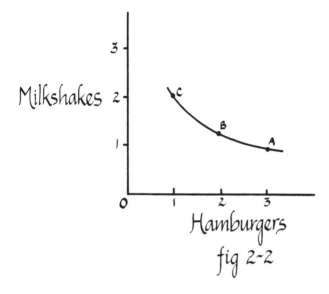

fig 2-2

Once we connect our three points representing combinations
A, B, and C, we then have a smooth curve showing *all* the "points
of indifference." In other words, if you should ask me, "Where
would you prefer to consume; at A, B, or C, or somewhere in
between?" I would have to answer that question by saying, "I'm
indifferent; that is, all points give me equal satisfaction."

Notice that my indifference curve in Figure 2-2 might be
described as having a "bow-like" shape. More precisely,
economists say that this indifference curve is *convex to the origin*
where the "origin" is always the lower left-hand corner. You may
wonder why my indifference curve (or any other one, for that
matter) has this general shape—i.e. why isn't it a straight line or in
the shape of a "dome?" The answer to this question lies in understanding our "new friend," the law of diminishing marginal utility.
Let's see how this works.

Look closely again at combination A, for example; it represents 3 hamburgers and 1 milkshake. If I happen to be consuming
at point A, I am obviously "full" of hamburgers. Recall that this
third hamburger added very little to my overall satisfaction. Since
this third hamburger is not that important to me, I'm going to be
willing to "trade it off" or substitute for it only a quarter of a

milkshake if I move to combination B. Also keep in mind that at point A, milkshakes *are* dear to me since I'm only consuming one of them. Because each fraction of a shake is giving me "so much pleasure," I'm unwilling to trade it off so readily.

But now let's look at combination C on Figure 2-2. Here, hamburgers suddenly become much dearer to me while milkshakes are well into their diminishing utility. Thus at point C, I am willing to forego *more* milkshakes if I desire to gain more hamburgers by moving on to point B. It is this difference in my desire to substitute milkshakes for hamburgers that gives this indifference line its unique shape.

In mathematical terms, we could say that the *slope* at point C is greater (i.e. steeper) than it is at point A. Economists call the slope at any given point *the marginal rate of substitution* (MRS). The MRS represents the number of milkshakes (or any other product that might be on the y axis) that must be substituted to get an additional hamburger (or any product on the x axis). Thus, as we gain more hamburgers, the MRS (and the slope) falls as we become less and less willing to substitute milkshakes for an additional hamburger. This falling slope can easily be seen in Figure 2-3.

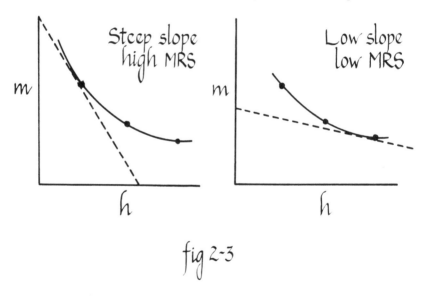

fig 2-3

There is, in fact, another way of determining the slope of my indifference curve in the foregoing example. All we need to do is take the ratio of the marginal utilities, i.e.:

$$\text{Slope} = \frac{MU_h}{MU_m}$$

This equation is somewhat difficult to prove mathematically, but we can easily reason out how it works using the law of diminishing marginal utility. For example, combination C represents a high marginal utility for hamburgers (i.e., few hamburgers consumed), and a low marginal utility for milkshakes. This situation thus gives us a high ratio and hence a steep slope:

$$\frac{MU_h \ (high)}{MU_m \ (low)} = \text{high ratio} = \text{high slope}$$

Of course, at combination A, everything is reversed, giving us a very low slope.

Having followed the discussion so far, you should be getting a feeling for the indifference curve—and more specifically *my* indifference curve for hamburgers and milkshakes. We realize, however, that *your* indifference curve might be entirely different. If for example, you happened to be a "milkshake freak" while you were "so-so" about hamburgers, your indifference curve would probably be much flatter than mine, implying that it would take many hamburgers for you to trade-off even a little bit of your milkshake. Thus, your curve might look something like the one in Figure 2-4.

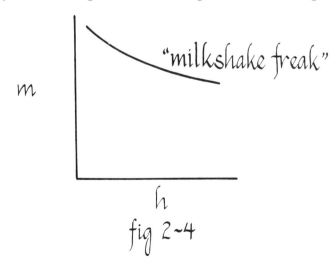

fig 2-4

Needless to say, we could draw thousands of different indifference curves which would reflect the unique consumption preferences of different individuals. Even for a given individual, we could show many different levels of utility. So far, we have only discussed a single indifference curve that represented a total amount of utility at the "Y" level. But there is also a curve somewhere below the "Y" level that would represent a lower total level of satisfaction—let's call it the "X" level—and another indifference curve even higher than "Y" which we might call total utility "Z". These different levels of utility which can be represented by a series of indifference curves are called *an indifference map*. My indifference map for milkshakes and hamburgers is shown in Figure 2-5.

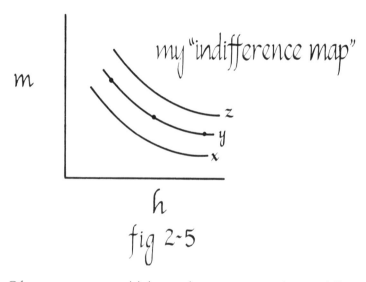

Of course, we *could* have drawn many other indifference curves—ones above and below and between those drawn in Figure 2-5. For simplicity's sake, we will show only the three, x, y, and z.

One important advantage of using an indifference map over our earlier approach is that with indifference curves, we are no longer compelled to attach actual utility values to the consumption of different products. For example, we really do not know how many "units of utility" are involved on the x curve. But we can still say with some certainty that x indifference curve is lower than y and if all other things were equal, one would rather consume on the higher curve (assuming that *more* goods are better than *less* goods). Of course, the highest state of satisfaction would be for me to move up to indifference curve z.

Now if things were absolutely free—i.e., we had no economic problem to solve—we surely would not hesitate to "climb" up to the highest indifference curve possible. But, of course, things are not free; we are forced to make painful choices because of our limited amount of income. Goods and services cost money, and we all have a limited income. This is the crux of the "economic problem." Is it possible to integrate the reality of product prices and one's income-constraint with our indifference curve analysis? Fortunately the answer is "yes." It can be done by drawing what is called a "budget line". Let's see how this works.

The Budget Line—

To show how a budget line works, let's go back to the earlier example where I was given an income of $4 per day, and also where the prices of both hamburgers and milkshakes were $1 each.

Now if I spent all of my $4 income on hamburgers (i.e., no milkshakes), I *could* buy 4 hamburgers. This means that my $4 budget gives me the opportunity of consuming at that point where we have 4 hamburgers and 0 milkshakes. We might mark this as one point on my budget line. Of course my $4 could also buy 2 hamburgers and 2 milkshakes or 3 hamburgers and 1 milkshake. These combinations, in turn, all represent *possibilities* of consumption given my $4 income and the dollar price for either product. In plotting these possibilities, I have, in effect, a budget line that shows every combination of hamburgers and milkshakes that can be bought for $4. Figure 2-6 (page 20) shows my $4 budget line.

Sometimes it's helpful to see a budget line like the one in Figure 2-6 as a kind of "economic straight-jacket"—a visual representation of the "cruel" world of economic reality. Of course, we would all like our budgets to be larger, but they are not, and once we've been allowed just so much income, we must limit ourselves to the consumption possibilities that lie somewhere on this line.

Yet, even though we are limited by this restricted budget, we still have a certain amount of *choice* in terms of selecting the *right*

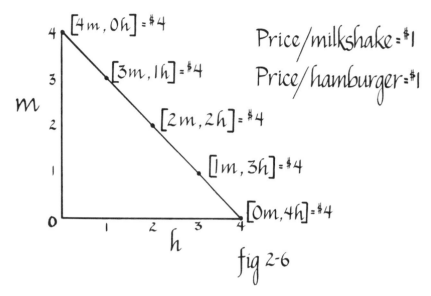

$$[4m, 0h] = \$4$$
$$[3m, 1h] = \$4$$
$$[2m, 2h] = \$4$$
$$[1m, 3h] = \$4$$
$$[0m, 4h] = \$4$$

Price/milkshake = $1
Price/hamburger = $1

fig 2-6

bundle of goods that will give us the greatest satisfaction. This is nothing more than the so called "economic problem" that we discussed earlier in this chapter. But how is the problem solved? How can we be sure that we have made the best choice with our $4 income?

To answer those questions, all we need to do is combine the budget line with the indifference map. The combined "system" can be seen in Figure 2-7.

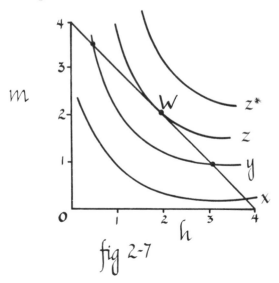

fig 2-7

The solution to my economic problem can be seen by analyzing the information in Figure 2-7. First note that it is *possible* to consume on indifference curve y. It crosses the $4 budget line in two places. But why should I stop on indifference curve y when it's possible to climb up to indifference curve z? Notice that there is *one* point where the budget line is just tangent to indifference curve z. This point of tangency represents the approximate consumption of 2 hamburgers and 2 milkshakes.

Yet, someone might logically ask, "If higher indifference curves represent higher satisfaction, why not go on to the highest indifference curve of all; i.e., that of z*?" The answer is, of course, that z* is not consistent with the $4 budget constraint. There is no point where the highest indifference curve coincides with the budget. The very highest possible level of utility attainable with the $4 budget is represented by that point of tangency, W in Figure 2-7. We have thus discovered a "graphical solution" to the economic problem:

> —the individual maximizes his (or her) utility by consuming at that point where the indifference curve is tangent to the budget line.

It does not matter whose indifference map we are looking at, nor does it matter what the dollar income constraint is. It does not matter, either, which kinds of goods and services we are looking at. One will always maximize total utility at the point of tangency. This is an extremely important conclusion—a conclusion that will take us to the very heart of the demand curve in the next chapter.

Chapter 3
Demand

Our goal in Chapter 2 was to develop a simple model of consumer "efficiency" making use of the indifference curve-budget line system. Figure 3-1 provides a summary of our conclusions. The smiling man shows us that point at which the consumer is maximizing his utility under a budget constraint. Note that we have used more generalized notations (i.e., instead of hamburgers we have used "good x," and instead of milkshakes, we have used "good y").

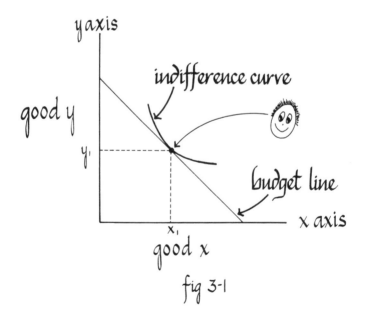

fig 3-1

Chapter 3 is devoted to *using* this kind of graphical approach to show a variety of economic relationships. I'll bet that you will be somewhat surprised to see how versatile this indifference curve system can be in describing consumer behavior under a variety of circumstances. Our *ultimate goal for this chapter is to derive a demand curve*; but first, let's look at some basics.

Income change—

Let's begin with an interesting situation where we change the income of an average consumer and see how this income change will affect his spending patterns. Let's call this person Chester Olson. We shall refer to him often during the rest of this book.

First, how might we show an "income change" on Chester's indifference curve graph? To see how this is accomplished, let's take a simple example in which Chester's income increases from $4 to $8 per day. Obviously, such an income increase can be represented by an "outward" shift in his budget line. Keeping the price of the "x" good (as represented on the bottom axis) at $1, and also the price of the "y" good at $1, the *new* points of reference with the $8 income on the x axis will now be 8 units of x. This means that if Chester spent all his income on x, he would be able to buy 8 units. Obviously if he spent the $8 all on y, he could also buy 8 units of y. In Figure 3-2 we have drawn a comparison between the old and the new budget lines.

Now let's take a variety of income levels and then examine the points of tangency with the indifference curves. In Figure 3-3a, these points of tangency tell us exactly where Chester will maximize his satisfactions at different levels of income.

In Figure 3-3b, we have connected all the points of tangency with a continuous line. This line is frequently called *the income consumption curve*. Just a "glance" at the income consumption curve will show the relative preference between the two goods as Chester's income expands. In Figure 3-3b, it looks as if Chester's preferences are fairly "balanced" between the two products. But this may not always be the case, as we shall soon see.

Income elasticity

"Income elasticity" is an interesting idea which, generally

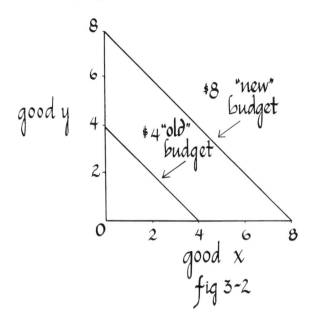

fig 3-2

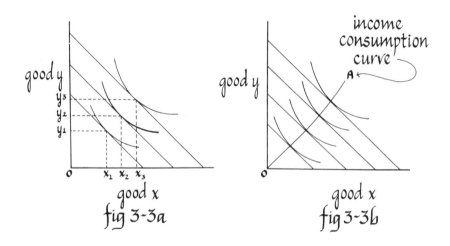

fig 3-3a   fig 3-3b

speaking, refers to how our spending changes as our income changes. A product that is highly income elastic, for example, would indicate that we would *greatly* enlarge our buying of it if our income went up. More precisely, our consumption of an income elastic good would go up *proportionately more* than our income. This means that the following ratio would be greater than 1:

$$\frac{\% \text{ change in x product}}{\% \text{ change in income}} > 1$$

On the other hand, an *income inelastic* product would imply a ratio of *less than one*. Let's look at an example of an inelastic product. It is generally thought that food, as a general category of products, is inelastic. This means that if my income doubled, my consumption for food products would *not* double. Our indifference curve system can show this relationship quite easily.

To see how this works, let's once again return to Chester Olson's situation where we doubled his daily income from $4 to $8. And instead of "x good" let's plug in "food" so we can observe what happens to his food consumption when we raise his income. In Figure 3-4a, we can easily see that Chester is reluctant to double his food consumption from the doubling of his income. And just to double-check our conclusions, we have drawn a $2 budget line to see if food remains an inelastic product at low income levels.

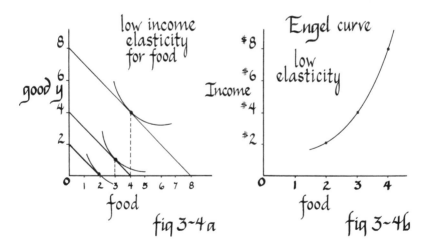

fig 3-4a   fig 3-4b

Sure enough, food for Chester Olson remains an inelastic product throughout the three levels of income. How can we be sure? Simply "dot" down to the x axis (food) and read off how much food he purchases at each income level. As you can see, a $2 income brings in about 2 units of food, at $4 Chester buys 3 units, and at $8, he buys 4 units. Although the income has doubled—and then doubled again, Chester's food consumption has simply not kept pace. This income inelastic characteristic of food is one of the sources of our so-called "agricultural problem" (which we will be discussing in Chapter 6).

Sometimes it is useful to graph income levels *directly* against product consumption as we have done in Figure 3-4b. This special relationship as represented by the curve shows the relative elasticity of a product at a glance. The curve itself is frequently referred to as an Engel curve* Thus, the Engel curve we have drawn for Chester Olson's food consumption is a steeply rising one— implying a low income elasticity—and by plugging in the numbers that we obtained from Figure 3-4a, we can see that it is actually inelastic.

Food as a general product category probably is inelastic. Yet, there may be certain areas of food consumption which might turn out to be just the opposite. For example, I know a number of people who love to eat in restaurants. They do not do it very often because eating out is a "luxury" in relation to their budgets. Thus, a doubling of their incomes may well bring about *more* than doubling of restaurant food consumed. If this indeed occurs, we would then be talking about an *income elastic* product. Let's take a moment to see how this situation might look on our indifference system and also on an Engel curve.

In Figure 3-5 (page 27) we have doubled Chester Olson's income twice—just as we did before; but this time we observe that the Olson family has *more* than doubled its consumption of restaurant food. Note also the Engel curve in Figure 3-5b. Again, by plugging in the actual consumption data derived from the indifference curve system, we see that "eating out" is an income elastic product for the Olson family since the percent change in "restaurant food" is greater than the percent change in income.

The Inferior Good—

We have talked a lot about food so far. Perhaps you are getting a little tired of the subject . . . or more likely, you may be experiencing a growing hunger for hamburgers, milkshakes, or whatever. But before you take off to the nearest restaurant, let me offer

---

*The Engel curve was named after a German economist, Ernst Engel.

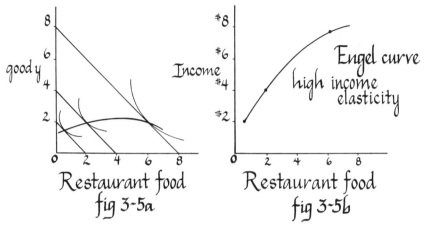

Restaurant food
fig 3-5a

Restaurant food
fig 3-5b

you one more example, one that is guaranteed to fascinate you. We call it *the inferior good.* But first a little background.

Up to this time, we have been discussing products that fall under the general description of *normal goods.* By definition, a normal good is a product or service which you will buy *more* of when your income increases (or less of, when your income falls).

But there is another whole category of goods, the inferior goods, of which the opposite is true; that is, when your income increases, you purchase *fewer* inferior goods. What are some examples? Potatoes are often cited as a good example of an inferior good, as is powdered milk. Please note, however, than an "inferior good" is not necessarily inferior in terms of quality or nutrition. Its "inferiority" is often only psychological. In this respect, an inferior good might also be called a "poor person's product" since families will tolerate the product at low income levels, but as their incomes rise, they discard the inferior in favor of "normal" goods.

How might we show this unique relationship between income and consumption of an inferior good? Let's go back to Chester Olson's indifference curve system to see; only this time, we'll put inferior good "potatoes" on the x axis (Figure 3-6a), and we will also see what happens if we put another inferior good (powdered milk) on the y axis (Figure 3-6b). Figure 3-6 is on page 28.

Note how the income consumption curve for potatoes in Figure 3-6a tends to bend backward—indicating that fewer and fewer potatoes are consumed as the income increases. On the other hand, if our inferior good is on the y axis, we see an income consumption line that bends downward.

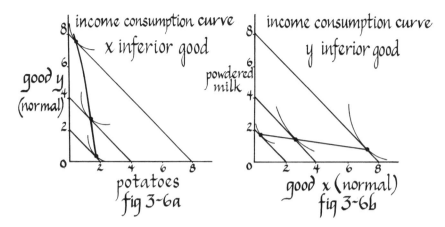

fig 3-6a

fig 3-6b

And finally, it might be useful to see what an inferior good might look like as an Engel curve. As you might expect, the "inferior Engel curve" looks a little like a downward sloping demand curve—but in this case, Figure 3-7, it's showing an inverse relationship between income change and the consumption of the inferior good.

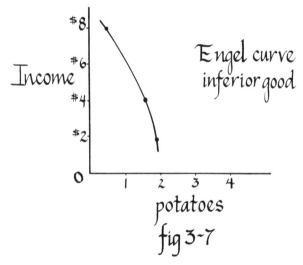

fig 3-7

Changing prices—

Income changes, such as we have been discussing above, are interesting; but they do not help us get to the heart of the demand curve which is our major goal for this chapter. What then is the important variable in understanding the concept of demand?

To answer this question, it might be helpful to review what a demand curve is all about. Demand, as you probably recall, is a relationship between *the price* of a good and the *quantity purchased* of that good. Can we derive a demand curve for hamburgers using our old friend Chester Olson as an example?

The easiest method is to put on our "economist-reporter" caps and simply *ask* Chester how many hamburgers he will buy at different hamburger prices. Let's say that he tells us that he would buy 1 hamburger if the price were $2, 2 hamburgers if the price went down to $1, and if the price were lowered to 50 cents, he would buy 4 hamburgers.

Thus our "direct research" method of finding out Chester's hamburger demand gives us the curve shown in Figure 3-8.

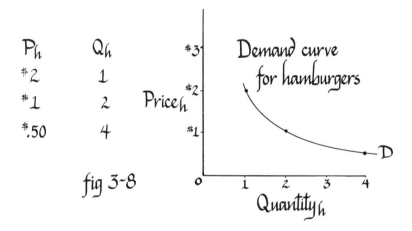

Another method of finding Chester's hamburger demand (the method we are in fact most interested in) would be via the indifference curve system. Of course, we must first find out what Chester's indifference map looks like for hamburgers; then all we have to do is *change the price of hamburgers* and observe how these price changes affect his hamburger consumption. How can we "make a price change" on our indifference curve-budget line graph?

To see how this might be done, let's go back to our old example of a $4 budget and an original price of hamburgers at $1 apiece. Let's now decide to lower the price to say 50 cents and see what happens to Chester's budget line.

At 50 cents a hamburger, Chester's $4 income can now buy a maximum of *eight* hamburgers. More generally, we can easily determine where the budget line will intersect the x axis by dividing the income by the price of the hamburgers; i.e., Income/P_h. Thus, if hamburgers happened to go up to $2 apiece. Chester could buy a maximum of only 2 hamburgers with his $4 income ($4/$2 = 2).

Therefore, *each time the price of hamburgers changes, the budget line will change its slope.* At lower hamburger prices, it will generally have a low slope, and at high prices for hamburgers, the budget line becomes steeper. (We are assuming, of course, that there is no price change with the "y" good). You can check out the slope changes in Figure 3-9.

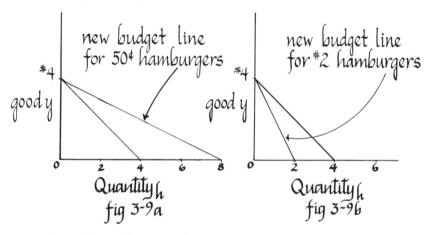

Now all we have to do is add Chester's indifference curve map—i.e., those indifference curves that happen to be tangent to the different budget lines. When we connect these points of tangency with a line, we have what is commonly called a *price consumption curve.* This curve can be seen in Figure 3-10a.

Deriving the Demand Curve—

Now we can say (without appearing too melodramatic) that we are nearing a kind of "climax" for this chapter. In other words, after our long labors of analysis, we are coming very close to that point where we can derive a demand curve from our indifference curve system and our price consumption curve.

In fact, the last connecting link is really quite simple; perhaps

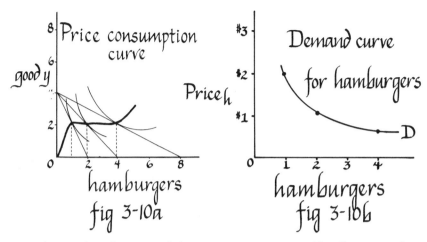

fig 3-10a

fig 3-10b

you have already spotted the connection yourself. All we need to do to find points on Chester's demand curve is to read off the number of hamburgers that he will consume at the different prices of hamburgers (Figure 3-10a). Thus, at the $2 price, (the steepest budget line), we see that Chester will "demand" about 1 hamburger. Then lower the price to $1 (the middle budget line) and we see he will want 2 hamburgers. And finally, if we "dot" down to the hamburger axis from the point of tangency of the lowest sloped line (representing 50 cent hamburgers), we see that Chester will demand 4 hamburgers. These results, as summarized by the demand curve in Figure 3-10b, are, in fact, in exact agreement with our simpler method of finding demand via direct research. (See Figure 3-8.) The difference in methods of finding Chester's demand are both valid—but the one using the indifference curves took us way back to the very beginning assumptions of consumption (remember the law of diminishing marginal utility?) and was built up, in a sense, "from scratch."

Let's now examine a more generalized situation, using the universal notation of "x good" instead of hamburgers, and "P" for prices. In Figure 3-11a and b (page 32), we see a generalized demand situation as we change the price of x good from P_4 down to P_1.

Thus, Figure 3-11b represents our first general demand curve—our very own—based upon indifference curve theory! In that we have now completed one-half of a simple market (the demand half), this represents a major accomplishment.

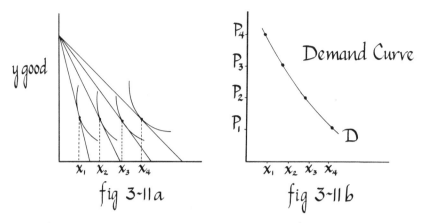

fig 3-11a   fig 3-11b

There is now only one more task for us to do to complete our theory of demand; we must learn about what are called the "income and substitution" effects. Let's see how they work.

Income and Substitution effects—

What do we know about the nature of demand? In its simplest form, demand is nothing more than the inverse relationship between the price of a good and the quantity demanded. That is, as we reduce the price of x good, we observe that an individual will increase his or her quantity demanded for that product—say from quantity X₁ to quantity X₂. OK, fair enough; there doesn't seem to be anything so unusual about that—it's what we have been discussing all throughout this chapter.

What we have not discussed, however, is exactly *why* a person tends to want more of a given product at the lower price. Why this is so is really quite interesting.

We have found that there are actually *two* separate "effects" that encourage a consumer to buy more of a product at the lower price. One is called the "income effect" and the other, the "substitution effect." Let's first take a look at the substitution effect.

Imagine that we have an indifference curve that represents two substitute goods—say, coffee and tea. Now imagine that all of a sudden the price of tea drops to a very low level, while the price of coffee remains at a relatively high level. Thus tea is now *relatively less* expensive than coffee and would thus encourage you to purchase more tea. What really happens, of course, is that now you can gain a *greater amount of utility* by purchasing tea because of its cheaper price. The graphic result of the lower tea price is that the consumer would move *along his indifference curve* to a point that favored more tea.

The "income effect" is a little different. Here the consumer observes a fall in the price of tea and says to himself, "What a pleasant surprise — with the drop in tea prices, I am now a little bit richer — I have more purchasing power (i.e. "real income") to spend on everything I enjoy."

Of course, if tea is a *normal good,* he will spend *some* of his extra real income on tea. Thus, a little bit of the overall increase of tea consumption comes from this *income effect.*

Both the income and substitution effects can be shown on our indifference curve system. Let's assume that we reduce the price of good "x" and that there is a total increase in consumption from x_1 to x_2. Our graphical representation will show us exactly how much of this total increase was due to the income effect and how much was due to the substitution effect. Let's check this out by first looking carefully at Figure 3-12.

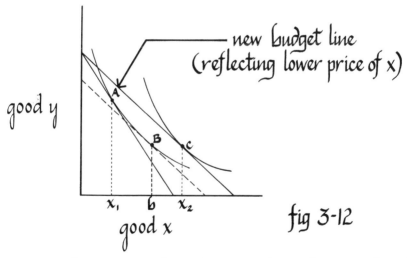

new budget line
(reflecting lower price of x)

good y

good x

fig 3-12

Note that our original situation was to lower the price of good "x" and then we observed that there was an increase in quantity demand from x_1 to x_2 or we might say, the horizontal distance from point A to point C. Thus A to C would be representative of the *total change.*

Next note the dotted "phantom" budget line. This line has been carefully drawn to be

a. tangent to the original indifference curve at point B
b. parallel to the budget line that represents a low price for "x."

Perhaps you can now guess what the "income effect" is. It is that increase in "x" from B to C which was a result of a positive change in real income. Recall that we have always represented income changes (i.e., budget line changes) by a *parallel* shift in the budget line (see Figure 3-2, for example). Thus, a shift from B to C (or from b to x₂) is due to the income effect.

The substitution effect is the amount of increase in "x" that is represented by the horizontal distance between A and B or between x₁ and b. As we discussed earlier, the substitution effect is a result of "moving-down" the original indifference curve; i.e., more of good "x" and less of the relatively higher priced substitute good "y."

To summarize: A to B is the substitution effect, B to C is the income effect, and both "effects" combined give the total increase from A to C (or from x₁ to x₂).

This pretty much completes our study of demand (whew!). We've learned where the demand curve comes from and we have also learned to do some very interesting things with income changes. In addition, we have moved a long way toward developing some valuable tools which should make the study of "production theory" much easier (particularly in Chapters 7 and 8).

But before we go on to the next chapter, which looks at the background to the supply curve, let us once again observe a simple demand curve—a more friendly curve now—to remind us how far we have come:

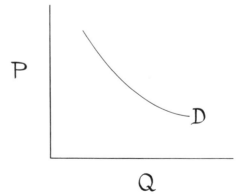

Chapter 4

Background to Supply; Pricing Resources

The Product Supply Curve—

Perhaps the supply curve is a familiar image to you. It's a line on a graph that is drawn upward to the right, representing a positive relationship between the price of a product and the quantity of output that producers wish to supply. The higher the price, the greater the quantity supplied, as shown in Figure 4-1.

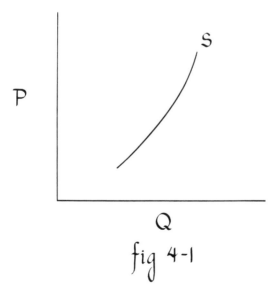

fig 4-1

But why does a supply curve have that particular shape? In introductory economics classes, we usually hear a common sense explanation that goes something like this: When farmer Brown sees a rise in the price of corn, he will logically want to supply *more* corn to the market, thus the higher the price of corn, the more corn...

Indeed, this is probably a true statement, but it certainly does not *prove* much. In order to really get at the true nature of a supply curve, we must first understand *how a producer maximizes profits.* Decisions on profitability will, in turn, take us into the financial regions where profits are determined—i.e., *revenues and costs of production.* Thus, let us begin our exploration of supply with the subject of production costs, for it is here that we learn what really goes on "behind the scenes" of an average supplier.

Costs of Production and Resource Pricing—

One interesting thing about product supply is that: when we think we have a handle on the right concepts, we suddenly find out . . . "not quite!" We find ourselves compelled to explain where *those* concepts came from, and then again, the origin of those earlier ideas on which the concepts are based.

For example, we know that "costs of production" play an important role in understanding profitability; but where do costs come from? Think about it for a minute. You're probably answering in your mind, "Costs obviously come from *resource markets;* i.e., the supply-demand situations for land, labor, and capital . . . from there we get resource prices, and from these prices, we derive costs."

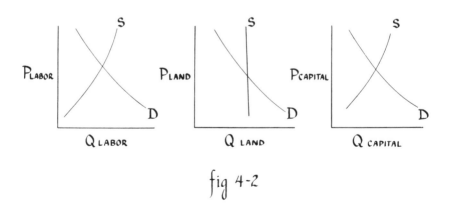

fig 4-2

You may even wish to show some sample resource markets like the ones in Figure 4-2 to indicate how these resource prices are obtained.

But we are still left with a puzzle, aren't we? In Figure 4-2 we have drawn supply and demand situations for the three major resou,ces, but what is the *origin* of these supply and demand curves?

Each question raises new ones, as we travel backward into the heart of microeconomic theory. It's a process that reminds me a little of Henry Thoreau's attempt to find a "bedrock point of departure" from which he would begin his philosophical search for truth:

> Let us settle ourselves, and work and wedge our feet downward through the mud and slush, . . . till we come to a hard bottom and rocks in place, which we can call reality . . . a place where you might found a wall or a state. (from *Walden*)

Can we find our own "bedrock" concept—a solid principle of production from which we can build our microeconomic wall?

I believe the concept we are looking for is *the law of diminishing returns* which is perhaps the most fundamental law in all economics. What exactly is this law all about? And how does it relate to resource markets and costs of production? Let's take a look.

Diminishing Returns—

I have always found it easiest to explain diminishing returns using an example from the farm industry. Let's take the baling of hay as a specific example. Hay-baling is a type of production that is fairly uncomplicated and that can be easily visualized. Let's take our consumer friend from Chapter 3, Chester Olson, and make him a *producer* of baled hay. Let's assume that Chester has a small farm of about 50 acres. We'll simplify Chester's situation slightly by saying that he has *fixed capital* consisting of one tractor, one baler, and one hay wagon. Keep in mind that whenever we discuss any diminishing returns example, we must always keep *all resources fixed except one.* Considering only one variable resource, economists say that Chester is operating in *the short run.* In contrast, the long run would be a situation in which Chester could change *all* his resources. We'll look at Chester's long run situation in Chapters 7 and 8, but for now, let's just consider him in the short run.

Thus, as economists, we have limited Chester's flexibility by allowing him only one variable resource. Which resource? For a farmer, the logical variable resource would be labor. Now let's see what happens as Chester adds different amounts of labor resource to his set of fixed capital and land resources.

We find that Chester, working by himself, is capable of bringing in 2 loads of hay a day. That does not seem like much. Of course, Chester is limited by the fact that he is doing all the work himself—baling the hay, taking the wagon out to the field, getting off the tractor, loading one bale of hay, getting back on the tractor, and moving on. And you are correct if this seems to you like an inefficient way of baling hay. Chester will face similar difficulties when he unloads and stacks the hay in the barn by himself. It's clearly *not* a very efficient one-man operation.

Let's assume that I join Chester, and that my contribution is an extra 3 loads of hay (i.e., the total for both of us would be 5 loads). The amount of hay that any one individual adds to the total is called that person's *marginal physical product* (MPP). Thus Chester's MPP would be 2 loads and mine would be 3 loads.

Note that we now are in a situation in which the marginal physical product is actually rising. This is exactly the same thing as saying, "we are experiencing increasing returns."

It's not difficult to see why we are in the stage of increasing returns. Chester's fixed resources are pretty much designed for 2 or more people. Simple efficiencies come about when one person can bale hay while another person can immediately stack the hay on the wagon. The same "two-man efficiency" takes place when the hay is unloaded and stacked in the barn.

But now what do you think will happen when Chester hires a *third* person? What do you think would be man number 3's marginal physical product in relation to the earlier workers?

What actually happened, when my cousin Steve helped, was that our daily total went up to six loads. Therefore, the extra output attributable (i.e., the MPP) to Steve is only *one* more load. Apparently, with the addition of the third worker, *MPP is beginning to fall* (recall that my MPP was 3 loads). A falling MPP, in turn, is telling us that we have now reached *the point of diminishing returns.*

Keep in mind that Steve's lower MPP was not because Steve was a less diligent worker than I. Steve's MPP was lower because we were all working with a limited amount of fixed inputs. One more tractor and wagon would have made a big difference in Steve's productivity. But alas, as a condition of diminishing returns, we can't change any of our fixed resources.

By the way, diminishing returns would also come about if we had held *labor and land constant* and then added more capital. Diminishing returns is a universal law that seems to work no matter what variable resource we happen to be looking at.

You may enjoy, as I do, thinking through different kinds of production processes such as farming, teaching, operating a restaurant—or even situations as varied as studying for an exam or operating a governmental department—and trying to imagine at what point diminishing returns is likely to set in. For example, in cramming for an exam, you might say, ''I seem to have reached the point of diminishing returns,'' implying that the most recent hour's worth of study brought in a smaller amount of knowledge than the previous hour's study.

Returning now to our example of Chester Olson, can we say that since Steve's low contribution results from diminishing returns, that Chester should *not* hire him? This is an extremely important question—a question, by the way, that will help us gain some insight into Chester's profitability decisions.

The answer to the above question will depend upon the monetary return from Steve's contribution compared to the wage that Chester has to pay him. Chester may indeed want to hire Steve if his contribution is worth more than what the daily wage rate happens to be. Let's take an example.

Recall that Steve's MPP was only one load of hay. But what if a load of hay were worth $50? The worth or value of Steve's MPP would be $50, wouldn't it? Economists call this amount *the value of the marginal product,* or just VMP. The VMP of any worker can easily be found by multiplying his MPP times the price of the final product;

$$VMP = MPP \times P_{hay}$$

Once Chester figures out what the VMP of *any* worker is, all he has to do is compare this amount with the wage paid to that worker. Thus, the general rule for Chester to follow in hiring workers is *to keep hiring people as long as the VMP is greater than the wage.*

In a way, this is like Chester Olson's *marginal decision making process* discussed in the last chapter. Recall that Chester took each dollar, one at a time, and asked where that dollar would give him the greatest utility.

Chester must also make marginal decisions, only this time in the following form, "Should I hire the first person (i.e., does he contribute to profits by bringing in a larger revenue than his cost)? . . . Should I hire the second person . . . Should I hire the third?" . . . and so forth. Each person must be a separate marginal decision based upon that person's contribution versus the wage that Chester will have to pay.

For example, should Chester hire me? Remember that my MPP was 3 loads. Thus at $50 a load, my VMP would be $150. We will now assume that Chester is paying "the going wage" of $20 per day.

Obviously, the worth of my contribution is far greater than the wage. Thus, in regards to me, Chester's marginal decision would be a resounding "yes."

Now to answer our earlier question about Steve. Steve's VMP was $50, and his wage is only $20. So even though diminishing returns sets in with Steve, it is *still* profitable to hire him (i.e., a $30 marginal profit).

What about a fourth person? Let's say that a fourth worker brings in one-half a load. Even with a low productivity as this, it is still worth Chester's while to hire another person. Why? Because man number 4's VMP ($25) is slightly greater than his wage ($20). Chester's marginal decision is now a more modest "yes" than before . . . but still a "yes." On the other hand, had the "going wage" been, say $30, there would have been no economic advantage to hiring the fourth person.

To maximize profits, it should now be clear that Chester should really keep hiring people *right up to that point where the VMP equals wage.* Even if a worker's VMP were $20.01, and the wage were $20.00, there would still be a tiny profit involved—and thus Chester ought to hire him. This is a rule, or general principle which we will return to later as a "profitability shortcut."

This rule, in turn, can give us some insight into the nature of resource markets—and more specifically resource demand. Let's see how this works.

The Demand Curve for Labor—

What is a demand curve for labor? It is nothing more than a series of points that tells us how many units of labor (i.e., the number of workers) will be purchased (by the producer) at different labor prices (or wage rates). To help us see how the labor demand curve is related to our discussion of marginal physical product, let's graph Chester's MPP curve and the related VMP curve using the information that we discussed earlier:

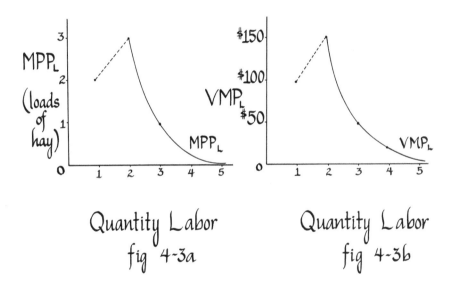

Quantity Labor
fig 4-3a

Quantity Labor
fig 4-3b

From the information in Figure 4-3, labor demand is really quite easy to work out. Choose any labor price or wage . . . say $25 per day. How many workers will Chester "demand" if the wage happens to be $25? The best way to answer this question is to go through the "marginal decision making" process that we discussed earlier; i.e., should Chester hire man number 1(himself)? The answer is "yes", as it would also be for workers 2, 3, and 4. Our short-cut method would give us the same results; that is, "hire up to that point where the VMP = wage." We see that a $25 wage will only equal a $25 VMP as the 4th man is hired. Therefore, one point on Chester's labor demand curve would be a $25 wage combined with 4 workers.

Now if the going wage were $50, Chester would hire up to and including man number 3 (remember that Steve's VMP was $50). Thus, Chester would have a second point on his labor demand curve.

And finally, with a wage rate of $150, it would obviously be worthwhile only to hire 2 people. This would make the third point on the labor demand curve. Below we have plotted these points in Figure 4-4a. And when the three points are connected as in Figure 4-4b, we have a complete demand curve for labor.

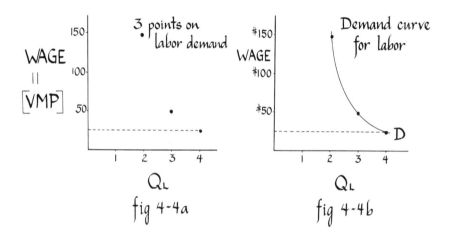

fig 4-4a   fig 4-4b

It should be no surprise that Chester's demand curve for labor looks exactly like the VMP curve for labor in Figure 4-3b. In fact, as long as Chester maximizes his profits where VMP = wage, then the VMP curve *will become* the labor demand curve!

Thus, our surprising conclusion is that *labor's demand curve is simply labor's VMP curve.* And the VMP curve is, in turn, a monetary representation of diminishing marginal physical product. Why then does the demand curve for labor slope downward? We now know it's because of declining MPP, or more simply, because of diminishing returns!

This conclusion is, in fact, true for *any* resource; i.e., the demand curve for capital or land is also *their* respective VMP curves in the short run. Thus, these other resources also have downward sloping demand curves which reflect *their* relationship to the law of diminishing returns.

So much for resource demand. But what about supply? If we are to discover the origin of resource prices (in order to understand costs), we've got to develop a supply curve to complete our resource market. So let's now take a look at what is behind a resource supply curve—and as before, we will spend most of our time looking specifically at the situation for the *labor* resource.

The Labor Supply Curve—

In my opinion, labor supply is one of the most interesting topics in microeconomic theory. It's interesting partly because it does *not* lend itself to a simple maximization process as did labor demand.

Instead, labor supply is conceived in man's inner psychological realm. It's a subject that addresses itself to different types of people, and their *unique* preferences for work and leisure.

How, for example, could we possibly explain via simple economic rules, one person's tendency to become a "workaholic?" Or, at the other extreme, how could it explain another person who takes his or her leisure when they feel like it; such as the individual in Robert Frost's "Lone Striker". In this poem, the subject, one fine day, simply refuses to supply his labor to the local woolen mill:

> He knew another place, a wood,
> And in it, tall as trees, were cliffs;
> And if he stood on one of these,
> Twould be among the tops of trees . . .
> He knew a spring that wanted drinking;
> A thought that wanted further thinking
> A love that wanted re-renewing . . .

Obviously, there are all types of work attitudes which we must take into consideration in discussing an individual's willingness to supply labor. And yet, I think that the *general configuration* of most people's labor supply curve would probably be somewhat similar. Let's try to figure out what that configuration is by use of an example.

Let's say that you wanted to find out what *my* labor supply curve looked like. You would probably begin your investigation by asking me a question like this, "Given complete freedom to choose the amount of hours you wanted to work, how many hours would you choose per week if you received $2 per hour?" The answer to that question would give you one point on my labor supply curve. Next, you might ask, "How many hours would you work if the wage were $3 per hour? . . . $4 per hour? . . ." and so on.

You may wish to inquire about my work preferences even at very high wages—and each time I answer, you note down the desired quantity of labor. No doubt my response to a rising wage rate would be similar to most people's response. If, for example, the wage were extremely low, I would probably be hesitant to "break my back" by working long hours—unless I were forced to by necessity.

But then as the wage increased, the possibilities for a greater income would probably be an incentive to put forth more hours. We might call this direct, or positive, relationship (i.e., higher wage rates leading to *more* hours worked), the *consumption effect*. This effect implies that a higher wage encourages me to increase my level of consumption at an accelerated rate.

However, at some high wage level, a remarkable thing happens. It suddenly occurs to me that "enough is enough," and that any higher wage after this point will result in *fewer* hours worked. Apparently I am now looking for a greater amount of leisure in which to enjoy my relatively higher income. When we observe this happening, we say that the *leisure effect** has become more powerful than the consumption effect.

What we have then is not just a positive slope to the labor supply curve, but also a slope that becomes "negative" when the leisure effect takes over. This makes the labor supply curve appear to "bend backward;" and hence, economists frequently refer to it as a *backward bending supply curve for labor*. This interesting configuration can be seen in Figure 4-5.

What makes this curve even more interesting is the fact that we can experiment around with different curve *shapes* to show a variety of work attitudes and work behavior patterns. Just for fun,

---

*Some textbooks call the *consumption effect* the "substitution" effect, and use the term "income effect" for what is called here the *leisure effect*. The change was made because the reader might easily confuse these terms with the "income effect" and "substitution effect" from the theory of demand in Chapter 3.

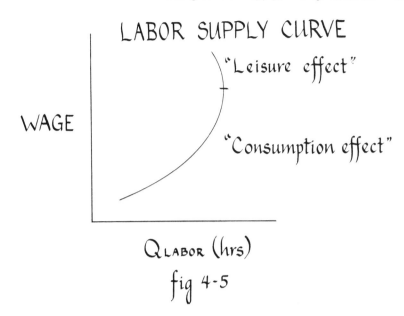

LABOR SUPPLY CURVE

WAGE

"Leisure effect"

"Consumption effect"

Q LABOR (hrs)

fig 4-5

let's try three radically different work models; first, the so-called "workaholic."

The workaholic's labor supply curve would probably demonstrate high initial work loads—which would increase *even more* as the wage rates increased. These kinds of people seem to need lots of work, and the possibilities for higher consumption levels prod them on as the wage increases. Thus, the leisure effect would only be evident after extremely high quantities of labor had already been supplied (see Figure 4-6a).

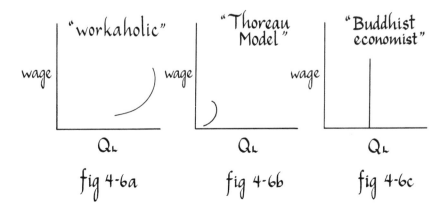

"workaholic"

wage

Qʟ

fig 4-6a

"Thoreau Model"

wage

Qʟ

fig 4-6b

"Buddhist economist"

wage

Qʟ

fig 4-6c

Next we will look at the "other end" of the work spectrum. For want of a better term, we will call this work pattern the "Henry Thoreau Model." In *Walden,* Thoreau advocated a simple, low-overhead life style. His greatest skill, he once said of himself, "has been to want but little." This philosophy led Thoreau to something that was not quite voluntary poverty, but was close to it:

> I found that by working about six weeks in a year, I could meet all the expenses of living. The whole of my winters, as well as most of my summers, I had free and clear for study. (from *Walden*)

What then would the "Thoreau Model" look like? Apparently, this type of supply curve would bend back very quickly—such as the one in Figure 4-6b.

A final labor supply model would be one that we have already described in an earlier chapter—i.e., the "Buddhist economist Model" based on E. F. Schumacher's description where an individual should not be motivated primarily by wages, but instead, work is simply put forth as one part of a dignified existence. Too much work would not be an ideal situation, nor would too little work. Thus, the Buddhist model supply curve would probably *not* have an upward slope . . . or a backward bending section either. It would rise in a straight line at the "ideal" level of work as shown in Figure 4-6c.

You might now wish to draw an approximation of *your own* labor supply curve. Of the above three models, which does yours most resemble?

A labor market—

So far we have examined a *single producer's* demand curve for labor, and a *single person's* labor supply curve. What we must do now is find out what the overall *industry* supply and demand curves look like.

Fortunately finding the industry supply and demand curves is not a particularly difficult job. For example, to determine the overall demand, all we need to do is ask all the hay farmers the same questions we have already asked Chester Olson; i.e., "How much labor would you demand at different wage rates?" If at a four dollar rate Chester maximizes his profits with x workers, and farmer Jones, y workers, and farmer Smith, z workers (and so on), then we simply add up the total numbers of workers ($x + y + z$ . . .

etc.) at that particular wage rate to get our first point on the industry demand curve (see point L₁ on Figure 4-7 below).

At a three dollar wage rate, we would go through the same addition process to obtain another point (L₂) . . . and then do the same for a two dollar rate (L₃). Connecting these three points, we have our *industry demand* curve for labor which would look something like Figure 4-7.

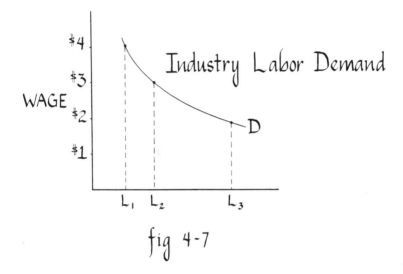

The supply curve for labor is determined in a similar way— i.e., we add up the total amount of labor that *all* workers (in that particular market) wish to put forth at the different wage rates.

On the next page, we have combined the industry labor supply curve with the industry demand curve. Together they form our first *labor market*—a unique supply-demand situation which generates its own equilibrium price (i.e., wage W₁) and its own equilibrium labor quantity (L₁) as can be seen in Figure 4-8.

All right then, for the labor market. But now what about the other resources—i.e., land and capital? What do their markets look like and how do we determine their prices?

Fortunately, we can apply a very similar kind of analysis to both land and capital. For example, the short-run demand curve for land is what you would expect—it's *land's value of the marginal product curve*. It slopes downward for the same reason that labor's demand did, diminishing returns.

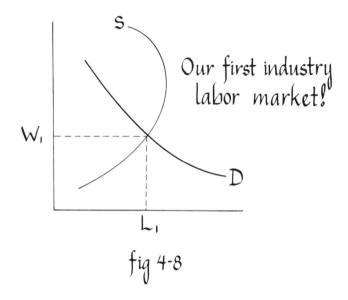

fig 4-8

The other half of a land market is land's supply curve. We know that by definition, the supply of land is fixed; i.e., there is only so much land resource—no matter what its price is. Thus, land's supply curve is simply a vertical line at the fixed quantity of land resource. The combined supply-demand market for land would therefore look something like Figure 4-9.

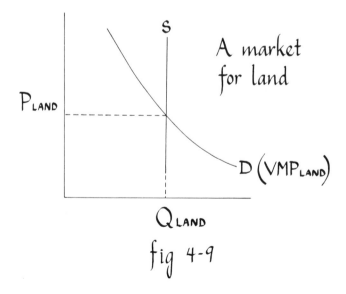

fig 4-9

And finally, let us look at capital. Capital's demand curve is its VMP curve too, and capital's supply is determined by the available capital stock at any one time. The resulting equilibrium price is often expressed as a rate of interest.* We will, however, use the designation "P capital" here to simplify our analysis in Chapter 5. Thus, a short-run market for capital would have the appearance of Figure 4-10.

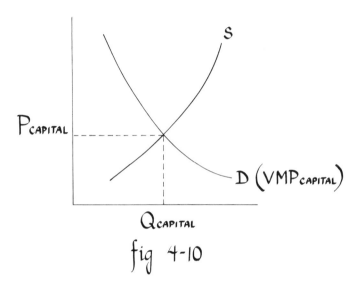

fig 4-10

We have now reached our major conclusion for this chapter on the "background to supply." We have traced short-run production theory from the basic principle of the law of diminishing returns through simple resource markets, and finally as we see above, we know *how the major resources are priced*—i.e., we know how an industry like farming obtains its prices for land, labor, and capital; and it is from these prices that we will ultimately determine a *producer's costs of production*. In the next chapter, it will be our job to combine costs of production with *revenues* in order to see how the producer maximizes profits. This knowledge, in turn, will ultimately lead us to *the product supply curve*.

---

*For further information on this subject, see Paul Samuelson's detailed discussion in Chapter 30, "Interest and Capital" in his textbook *Economics*, Tenth Edition, c 1976, McGraw Hill, New York.

Chapter 5

Competitive Supply

A review and a look ahead—

Let us take a minute now to look back and see how far we have come, and also to look ahead to where we are going.

First of all, we should remind ourselves of our primary objective for the first half of this book: to try to build a simple market model. That is, we have been exploring the origins of the familiar supply and demand curves that make up a typical competitive product market.

Chapter 2 and 3 covered the demand curve. The origin of demand, we learned, can be traced back to the law of diminishing marginal utility and the *consumer's* desire to maximize his or her utility within a limited income.

In seeking the origins of the *product* supply curve, we found that we had to go back a step to first learn about a producer's costs of production. These costs, in turn, are based upon the *markets for economic resources* (land, labor, and capital) and their resulting prices. We also found that these resource markets were explained primarily through the law of diminishing returns combined with the *producer's* desire to maximize profits.

What we have yet to do is make the important connection between these costs of production and the actual supply curve for a product. This connection, then, will be the primary objective of Chapter 5. Thus, by the end of the chapter, we should have a bona-fide *product supply curve* which, when combined with the demand curve of Chapter 3, will complete our major objective of "building a model for a product market" from scratch.

The Idea of Costs—

Based on our work in Chapter 4, we can now derive Chester Olson's basic costs of production. First, we must determine the "going" industry resource prices by observing the equilibrium of supply and demand within their respective markets. In Figure 5-1, we have drawn those markets and the resulting price for each of the resources (P_{land}, P_{labor}, $P_{capital}$).

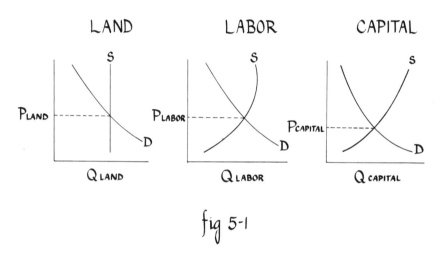

$$fig\ 5\text{-}1$$

Once these prices are known, we can begin to break them down into separate categories. These categories will eventually help Chester make his profitability decisions. Let's begin with Chester's "fixed costs."

Fixed costs—

Fixed costs result from the fact that we have been consistently describing Chester's hay operation as a *short-run* situation; i.e., land and capital are not allowed to change. The costs of these two resources, in turn, will be the "going" industry price (P) times the quantity (Q) of these resources that Chester decides to use. To illustrate this point with a very simple example, we'll say that his fixed costs are the following:

$$P_{land} \times Q_{land} = \$50$$
$$P_{capital} \times Q_{capital} = \$50$$

Adding these costs together, we have fixed costs of $100. Of course, we are greatly simplifying this point. In reality, Chester would have many many kinds of fixed or "overhead" costs on his farm. Land rental costs, tractor, wagon, baler, barn depreciation costs, insurance and taxes, are just a few examples of a typical farm's fixed costs.

Variable Costs —

In our example, Chester's variable resource is labor. Therefore, his variable costs would be the industry wage rate times the amount of labor that Chester decides to use (based on the procedures outlined in the last chapter).

Again, in reality, a farmer's variable costs are far more extensive than just labor. They would also include things like fuel, seed, fertilizer and so forth. In general, any raw materials that would be directly connected with output would have to be considered a variable resource.

To summarize Chester's situation in this example, we will say that his total costs so far will be the $100 fixed cost (FC) plus the variable costs (VC). Thus, his total costs = FC + VC. Indeed, these are the *obvious* costs to Chester and will generally involve an apparent outlay of money. Such apparent costs as these have a special name—they're called *explicit costs*.

There may, however, be another kind of cost—a cost not so obvious—which ought to be included as part of Chester's overall production costs. Economists call them *implicit costs*. Let's take a look at what this term means.

Implicit Costs —

Frequently, a single operator like our friend Chester Olson forgets to consider *his own labor* as part of his costs. Or more commonly, Chester will simply *undervalue* the long, long hours that he spends working on his farm.

This is also true with the many "ma and pa" stores, single proprietorships and partnerships—which often fail to fully recognize the value of the long hours spent on the job. Logically, we ought to include these kinds of "implicit" costs as part of the overall production costs.

How might we determine an implicit labor cost? In Chester's case, he could ask himself how much he might be able to earn elsewhere for working the same number of hours. Or an alternative method of finding an approximate value for his own labor is to ask himself how much he would have to pay someone else to replace him.

Note that if these implicit labor costs were actually included, it would have the effect of reducing what Chester had thought were his profits.

Another implicit cost that Chester has probably not fully accounted for is some fair *return* on his land and capital investments. If for example, he has invested $50,000 in farm assets, he is foregoing a certain rate of return he *could* be earning on this money in other forms of investment. (Indeed, even college students often forget to include this implicit cost when they figure out their overall costs for education!)

Thus, when economists look at "costs of production", they will include *both* implicit and explicit costs.

Social Costs—

Another category of costs which should be included (and usually is not) is what we call "social costs." Social costs are the financial sacrifices that society pays as a result of production. The most common form of social costs is *pollution* costs.

A good example of a social cost is when Chester Olson finds himself polluting his neighbor's water supply by extensive use of nitrogen fertilizer. This "nitrate poisoning" is a common problem in many rural areas. What usually happens is that when Chester's neighbors discover that their water is unfit for drinking, they go ahead and drill a deeper well at their own expense.

The economist looks at this situation (or any other pollution situation), and says that the financial cost of drilling a new well is really a legitimate cost of production for the farmer; i.e., Chester should really pay for this extra expense. Obviously we have a long way to go in recognizing the logic of social costs and also in forcing producers to *internalize* (that is, to bear the burden of) these costs themselves.

At any rate, when we now speak of "costs," we will be assuming that *all* legitimate costs will be included. Let's call the sum of these costs, the *total economic costs*:

EXPLICIT COSTS + IMPLICIT COSTS + SOCIAL COSTS = TOTAL ECONOMIC COSTS

Marginal Costs —

Taking into consideration all of Chester's economic costs, let's now look at an example of how costs change as Chester's output increases. We will assume that Chester can hire people even for a *part* of a day — so that he will be able to figure out *precisely* how much extra money it will cost him to produce one extra load of hay. Economists have a special name for this "extra cost of producing one more unit of output" — it's called *the marginal cost*.

For example, we might say that the marginal cost (MC) of the fourth load is $6, or the MC of the fifth load is $4. Once you know the total costs, the marginal cost is simply the *increment* between the various loads of hay. On the chart below, you can see how this works.

OUTPUT QUANTITY (loads)	TOTAL ECONOMIC COSTS	MARGINAL COSTS
1	$110	--
2	$130	$20
3	$140	$10
4	$146	$6
5	$150	$4
6	$170	$20
7	$210	$40
8	$270	$60

The next step is to graph the *marginal cost curve* using the data from the chart above. Chester's MC curve can be seen in Figure 5-2.

What does this MC curve show? It shows, at a glance, how much extra money it will cost Chester to produce any particular load of hay. One thing that stands out very clearly concerning the MC curve, is its interesting "U" shape. Apparently marginal costs first go down, and then around the fifth load of hay, they begin to go up. This common configuration implies that Chester must pay more and more money for extra loads of hay after the fifth load of hay. What do you think causes the MC to go down and then up?

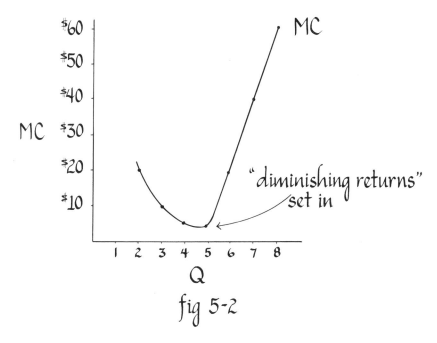

fig 5-2

Probably you have guessed the correct reason. It's our old acquaintance, "the law of diminishing returns." Recall that when Chester hired me, I brought the total daily production up to 5 loads. My MPP was 3 additional loads as compared to Chester's MPP of 2 loads. In other words, up to load 5, we were in the stage of "increasing returns" and thus my higher productivity led to *lower marginal costs.*

But to get an extra load after the fifth load of hay would become a very expensive proposition for Chester. Remember that Steve's MPP was only 1 load due to diminishing returns. But Chester must still pay Steve the same wage that he paid me ($20 per day). This explains why Chester's marginal costs literally "shoot-up" after this fifth unit, and also continue to rise rapidly from that point on. In short, the marginal cost curve begins to rise at that point where marginal physical productivity begins falling; i.e., where diminishing returns sets in.

We have now pretty much completed our analysis of short-run costs. It has taken up the good part of two chapters. Our most important conclusion so far has been the *derivation of the marginal cost curve* which has its origin in the law of diminishing returns. We know what the MC curve is, where it comes from, and why it is shaped as it is. We shall soon see that it is this "U" shaped MC curve that will eventually form the basis of the product supply curve.

But we still have yet one more important concept to pursue before we are able to put product supply all together; we need to know something about Chester's *revenues* as well as his costs to put the total "profitability" picture together. What then does our microeconomic theory tell us about revenues within the setting of a competitive market structure?

Let's answer this question by first defining what exactly we mean by the term "competition."

Competition—

What do economists mean when they use the term "competition?" I think the competitive market structure can be most easily understood as a marketing situation *precisely the opposite of a monopoly.*

Monopoly, of course, is the most concentrated market structure; competition, the *least* concentrated. A monopolist is a single seller of a product with virtually no substitutes (i.e., a "one-firm industry") and has undisputed control over industry price. In contrast, the perfect competitor is just one of many thousands or even hundreds of thousands of sellers; he is simply a drop in "an ocean of suppliers" who all supply ex*actly the same product.* In addition, the lone competitor has virtually *no control* over industry prices—nor is it worth his while to attempt to differentiate his product.

In one sense, "competition" is a confusing term. Ask the man in the street to name a competitive industry, and he might easily say "the automobile industry or the steel industry." Indeed, there may be a lot of *rivalry* between Ford and General Motors, but by our strict economic definition, they are not really competitive, since the auto industry does not adhere to the above competitive characteristics.

In addition, purely competitive industries have one attribute which auto manufacturers would never wish to share; *easy entry and easy exit.* Thus, to become a single seller in a true competitive market, we assume that you can move into the industry without a great deal of capital or exotic skills.

In turn, this characteristic of easy entry means that any excessive profit is threatened by new profit-seeking firms who easily move in, depress prices, and eventually squeeze out existing profits. This is the kind of "competition" which the large auto and steel industries wish to avoid.

Given all of the above characteristics, which industry in the United States would represent a competitive industry in your opinion?

The agricultural industry, in general, is often cited as a good example of a "competitive" industry. Of course, there are certain big business types of farms, such as a modern dairy farm, that are not so "easy to enter." In addition, the prices of certain grain crops have been supported by government programs which tends to dilute the "pure" competitiveness of modern grain-producing farms.

Perhaps a good example of farm competition is in hog or hay production. Hog producers, for example, *can* move into and out of the industry with relative ease. When prices are extra good, we see new hog producers moving in which helps eventually to lower the price of hogs. And once the easiest profits are achieved, many of the more inefficient producers leave the hog farming business as quickly as they originally moved in.

Now what about our earlier question concerning a competitor's revenues? Exactly how are revenues determined under competitive conditions? Generally speaking, the revenue situation for a competitor involves multiplying the industry price by whatever the competitor has to sell. For example, a single hog producer can sell 10 lbs or 10,000 lbs of pork *at the industry price*. No matter how much a single competitor has to sell, he cannot, in any way, affect the overall market price.

Since the above characteristics would also apply to hay producers, let us again return to Chester Olson to see if we can work out some general competitive principles using Chester as our primary example.

If Chester can sell all the hay he produces at the going price, what would *the demand curve* for Chester's product look like? Obviously the personal demand curve for Chester would be flat— or perfectly elastic—showing that the market will demand everything he produces at the industry price. In other words, if the overall market price for hay were $60 a load, Chester's own demand curve would look like Figure 5-3.

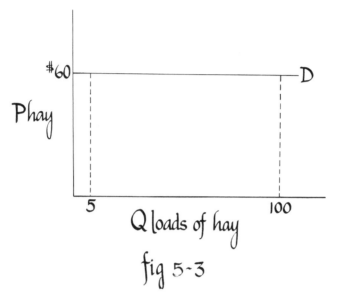

fig 5-3

    Once we know what Chester's revenue situation is like (as in his demand curve), we are then equipped with all the necessary information to complete our task for this chapter. All we must do now is connect up our knowledge of Chester's costs of production with his revenue situation to find out what his product supply curve looks like. Let's see how this can be accomplished.

Competitive Supply —

    To begin, let's review what we mean by the term "product supply curve." A product supply curve is a series of points that shows *how much output* a producer wishes to supply the market *at alternative prices* for that product. For example, Chester's supply curve for hay would indicate how many loads of hay he will supply if the going price of hay were say $60 a load . . . or $40 . . . or $20 . . . or any price in between. The line that connects up these points would thus become Chester's supply curve for hay.
    Obviously, Chester's decisions on "how much" hay to produce at different prices will be based upon *maximum profitability*. He will want to produce x amount of loads at $60 per load,

because x amount will give Chester the maximum amount of profits at that price. But exactly how will Chester *know* when he has arrived at that maximum profit quantity?

To find out the correct quantity, Chester must go through a marginal decision-making process that is similar to the one he went through when trying to decide how many workers to hire. But this time, he will be asking himself, "Will the first load be profitable? . . . will the second load be profitable? . . ." and so forth. Generally speaking, Chester should continue to add output as long as *each additional load keeps adding something to his profits.* To see how this works in more detail, let's return to our example.

Let's say that the market price of hay is $60 per load. Would it be profitable for him to produce the first loads of hay? The only way Chester can answer that question is to *compare the costs of those first loads with the revenues* he will receive by selling those loads. To find out what his costs are, he must refer to his *marginal cost curve* shown in Figure 5-4.

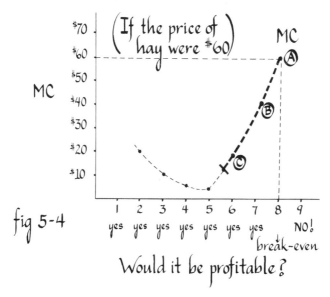

fig 5-4

Would it be profitable?

With the above MC curve, Chester will have very little problem making his "marginal decisions." Returning to our earlier question: Is it profitable to produce those early loads of hay? We can now see that the costs of production of the early loads are significantly *lower* than the $60 per load revenue he receives from selling those same loads. Thus, the answer is "yes."

But now let's keep moving along the x axis until we get to load #7. Again, Chester asks his marginal question, "Is it profitable to produce and sell unit #7?" From the graph above we see that load 7's marginal cost is $40, but the extra revenue continues to be $60; thus the marginal decision is still "yes." Now what about the 8th load? The 8th load is obviously a "break-even" situation—while any loads past 8, the MC will be greater than $60 and Chester should therefore not produce them.

Thus, if Chester follows the profitability rule of *producing up to that point where the price is equal to the marginal costs*; i.e.,

For Maximum Profit: Price = Marginal costs,

then Chester should stop right on the 8th unit if the market price were $60 a load. This information, in turn, gives us Chester's first point (point A) on his product supply curve.

To find another point on his supply curve, we would have to begin all over with a new price. For example, how much hay would Chester want to produce if the market price of hay were $40? Going through the same marginal decision process, Chester would obviously maximize his profits by producing and selling 7 loads. (Note that the 8th unit now would represent a $20 *loss*; its MC is $60, while the revenue is now only $40). A price of $40 and 7 loads supplied gives us Chester's second point on his product supply curve (point B).

Finally, if the price of hay were $20, we can easily see that Chester will stop producing with the 6th load (point C).

Perhaps you are noticing what seems to be a consistent pattern; i.e., the three points we have derived on Chester's supply curve are exactly the same three points on his marginal cost curve. Indeed, this is no mere coincidence, for it should now be apparent that *the competitive supply curve is nothing more than the producer's marginal cost curve.*

We should note, however, that if the industry price of hay falls *too* low, it may not be worth Chester's while to initiate production, at least in the short run. What do you think would be a "shut down price" for Chester? Before considering an example, let's recall what "short run" means. In terms of committing resources, "short run" means that our friend Chester could not get out of paying a fixed amount of fixed costs, even if he shut down his operation! Using the figures from our earlier example, we can say that the amount of money he would lose by shutting down would be his $100 fixed costs.

Now suppose that the price of hay fell so low that Chester's revenues would not even cover his variable costs. This would mean that poor Chester would lose not only the $100 fixed costs, but also would lose some money from the variable costs that were not matched by sufficient revenues. In this case, wouldn't it be wise for him to shut down and minimize his losses to the $100 fixed costs that are unavoidable in the short run? Sure it would.

Therefore, we can say that Chester's shut-down price is a price where the revenues generated from sales *will not quite cover variable costs*. Thus, our final conclusion concerning Chester's product supply curve is "the supply curve is the same thing as a producer's marginal cost curve *above the shut-down price.*" Chester's supply curve would therefore look something like Figure 5-5.

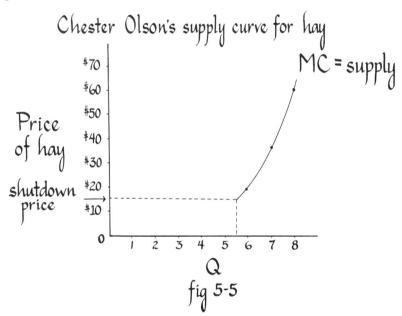

fig 5-5

With the derivation of Chester's supply curve, we are now near the completion of our journey. All we must do now is work out the so called "industry supply curve."

The industry in our simple example would include *all* producers of hay in that particular area. Therefore, to find the industry supply, all we do is add up the *total quantities of hay* that all producers wish to supply at the different prices. Indeed, the other producers' supply curves would probably look very much like Chester's because of similar marginal cost situations.

The only major difference between an individual's supply curve and the industry curve would be quantities of hay at the different prices. Thus, instead of 8 loads at $60, the industry might well produce *8 million loads.* Yet, the slope of the industry supply curve would obviously look very much like the positive sloped supply curve of Chester Olson.

Why, then, does the product supply curve slope upward to the right? Now we know for sure — it's because of rising marginal costs which, in turn, reflect *the law of diminishing returns.*

Building a Market —

So far we have used — perhaps overused — Chester's hay baling example to demonstrate the fundamentals of production. We have moved along with Chester from the basic law of diminishing returns, to resource pricing, to profit maximization on up to the derivation of the industry *supply curve.* Obviously, Chester and his fellow hay producers are just simple illustrations of what goes on "behind the scenes" of *all* competitive suppliers. Thus, in *any short-run competitive market*, the supply curve reflects rising marginal costs and therefore slopes upward to the right.

Similarly, we have also derived a simple *demand curve* in the early chapters of this book. In the case of demand, our starting point was the law of diminishing marginal utility which eventually contributed to a demand curve that was *downward sloping.* In turn, we can now say that *all* demand curves have a similar shape based on the theory of demand.

With both these theories of supply and demand behind us, it now seems like an opportune time to draw a *more generalized market* using a typical supply and demand curve from virtually any competitive market — we'll call it simply "industry x." That sample market is shown in Figure 5-6.

In Figure 5-6, we have thus completed our major objective of the first half of this book, i.e., *the building of a market.* We should, perhaps, stand back and admire this "basic building block" of our market economy . . . and when we look at it now, we can ap-

preciate, even more, the many principles and concepts that lie
behind those simple lines.

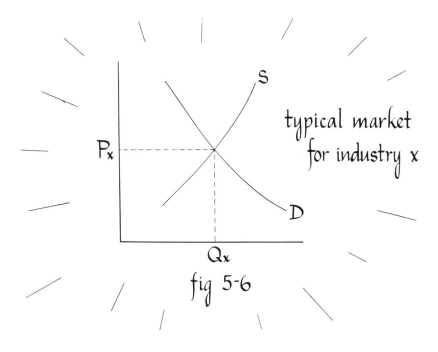

typical market
for industry x

fig 5-6

Chapter 6

Using the Markets

One of the enjoyable aspects of microeconomics is that after we have taken time and energy to build up a resource market or a product market, we then have at our disposal some tools that are more than "abstract" theory. These markets now become useful instruments which can help us understand *real-life* issues and problems. This chapter is devoted to examining some of these issues and problems.

The chapter is divided into two separate parts. Part I explores the uses of a typical *labor market* (as developed in Chapter 4). Specifically, we'll learn how labor markets can help us in understanding the problem of *income distribution*.

Part II uses our understanding of agricultural *product markets* (as developed in Chapter 5), to learn about the American farm problem. By this chapter's end, I hope that you will have gained a respect and an appreciation for the versatility and usefulness of these market models.

PART I—INCOME DISTRIBUTION—

Who receives the fruits of economic activity? Why do some individuals get more than others? What mechanism divides up society's income? What part of the economic pie will the labor resource get compared to capital or land resources? These interesting questions concern the topic of income distribution. Indeed, they are questions that have not always been easy to answer in relation to a modern market economy.

By contrast, in the age old *traditional economic systems*, where production and distribution were based upon well established patterns, the question of "who receives the output?" was easier to answer. Once you understood the culture's traditional source of power, which was usually based on land control, you pretty much understood how the income was distributed as well.

But what about our present market system? If traditional patterns do not determine "who gets the fruits of production," what does? A precise answer to this question—based on resource markets—was formulated around the turn of the century. The solution became known as the "Clark Theory of Distribution," named after the famous economist John B. Clark. Let's see what he had to say.

Clark's Theory of Distribution—

In its simplest form, Clark's theory attempted to demonstrate how much of the total economic pie went to the owners of *labor* resources as compared to that part of the pie that went to owners of *land*. His conclusion was, in fact, remarkably simple once one understood what was in back of a labor market. To demonstrate, let us redraw a typical labor resource market as we developed it in Chapter 4. Recall that the labor demand curve was largely a representation of worker's value of marginal product (VMP). We will simplify labor supply by using a vertical line as in Figure 6-1.

Clark observed that each worker will receive a wage only equivalent to that wage represented *by the last worker's value of marginal product*. In Figure 6-1, the eighth worker's VMP is $20. And it is at *that* point where supply crosses demand, and therefore *all workers* will receive a wage that is equivalent to the eighth (i.e., the last worker to be hired) worker's VMP. But notice that workers one through seven contributed much more than their $20 wage— but they *still* only get $20. Therefore labor's total share will be $20 x 8 workers, or $160 (which is represented by the shaded rectangle).

That takes care of labor's piece of the economic pie. But now, what about land's portion? According to Clark's analysis, the land-owner would receive what looks like a "surplus" represented by that area that is not shaded in. The unshaded triangle can be viewed as a value which the earlier workers contributed (i.e., their

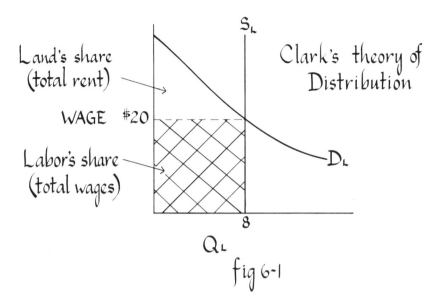

Land's share
(total rent)

WAGE $20

Labor's share
(total wages)

Clark's theory of
Distribution

fig 6-1

VMP is greater than their $20 wage) for which they did not get paid. In a pure market economy, the unshaded triangle represents a kind of *rent* or "return" to the owners of the land resource.

It should be obvious that labor's *wage rate* (and its share of the total economic pie) will be highly dependent upon the *positioning* of the supply and demand curve. This knowledge, in turn, can help us explain some very strange things that take place in our market economy—i.e., why do very hard working individuals frequently receive the lowest wages? Based on our understanding of resource markets, we can now explain this phenomenon very easily. Let's look at a typical example of this problem, which, for want of a better phrase, we'll call "the case of the waitress and her dentist."

The Waitress and Her Dentist—

Marilyn Jones, waitress at the Bixby drive-in, had to see her dentist, Dr. Franklin, last week. When she received her bill in the mail, Marilyn was at first surprised, then angered to discover that, in 30 minutes, her dentist had completed $50 worth of work—or about 3 full days worth of waitress' wages. "How could my dentist make forty to fifty times my own hourly wage?" she wondered.

This large differential in wages can be explained in large part by simple resource market analysis. To demonstrate, we have drawn a market for both dentists and waitresses, which we should look at carefully.

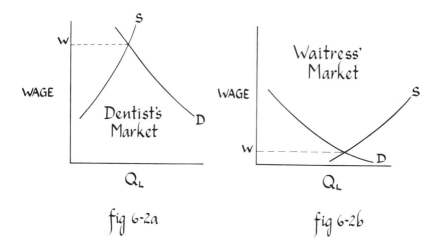

fig 6-2a   fig 6-2b

Let's look at the waitress market first. In Figure 6-2b, you can actually *see* how the supply-demand configuration works to the detriment of Marilyn Jones' wage rate.

Of course, just "looking" at the above market does not explain *why* the labor supply is so great, nor the demand so small. Let's examine some possible explanations for this unfortunate situation. First, let's look at supply. Why is it so large?

—too many relatively unskilled individuals who are willing and able to do this kind of work.
—relatively free entry into the waitress labor market; i.e., no unions, no licensing, no certification, etc. required.

The waitress labor market also suffers from too little *demand* relative to supply. What could cause this? Possible reasons, based on our knowledge of labor demand, are:

—the value of waitress' marginal product (i.e. their productivity) is low compared to a dentist's VMP . . . waitress work is labor-intensive with little use of technology or capital.
—the demand for the "final product" (i.e. a restaurant meal) is generally low in relation to the potential supply of waitresses.

On the other hand, Dr. Franklin's dentistry market (Figure 6-2a) has a more favorable supply-demand configuration—a high demand for dentist's labor, and a relatively low supply. What are possible explanations for this situation? First, consider the low supply:

—there are few qualified dentists relative to demand because of long and expensive training.

—restricted entry into the field . . . entrants are controlled by the professional associations who also control licensing exams, certifications requirements and so on.

And on the *demand* side, dentists benefit from the following factor, among others:

—dentist's productivity (VMP) is relatively high through the use of expensive dental technology (high-speed drills, x-ray equipment, etc.)

We should therefore keep in mind that high wage rates come about only as a result of *both* labor supply and labor demand being in favorable positions.

By the way, if by some quirk of fate, the waitresses in our above example had imposed stiff schooling and licensing requirements—while dentists had "opened-up" their profession by building more dental schools and by lowering some of the barriers to entry—then the gross wage differentials between these occupations would undoubtedly be reduced.

The above reasons are the *market* reasons why wages might differ. Of course, in the real world, there might be other explanations why one occupation, or one individual might suffer in relation to another. For one thing, waitress work has usually been considered "women's work," and as we know, traditional female occupations such as teaching, library work, nursing, etc. have historically been underpaid.

Another social factor that enters into a particular individual's wage is whether that person was fortunate enough to have had wealthy parents who could pay for expensive professional training. Also, "who you know," or "just plain luck" can play an important part in determining an individual's lifetime earnings.

Yet, the clearest and most precise reasons for large wage or salary differentials are the market explanations; indeed, explaining the issue of income distribution is one of the most useful applications of our theory.

Unions—

Another related area where we can apply our understanding of resource markets is the subject of unions.

Generally speaking, unions are formed because of an inherent weakness of individuals in dealing with very large, powerful, and often impersonal employers. Where single workers might be unsuccessful in promoting their individual interests, a unified group—with the power to strike—can usually promote the group's interests quite effectively. What is often overlooked when discussing unionization is how this organizational power can be directed toward the "manipulation" of labor markets; usually for the express purpose of raising the wage rate. We now have an excellent background to understand how this is accomplished.

There are basically three techniques by which organized groups can raise their wage rates. Let's begin with the shifting of the labor supply curve. Note Figure 6-3.

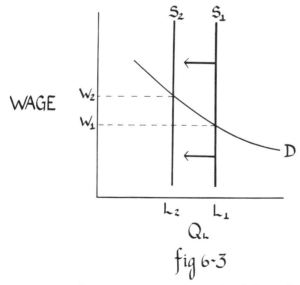

fig 6-3

A question that arises is, "How is this leftward shift in supply accomplished?" Fortunately, we have, in fact, already touched upon some of the methods. For example, any organization that

erects stiff barriers of entry...or simply upgrades entry requirements, will have the effect of shifting labor supply to the left.

In this respect, we see a large variety of professional
organizations—from barbers to doctors to teachers and account-
ants—insist upon various degrees of schooling and also the taking
of state licensing examinations before they allow an individual to
practice.

Other labor organizations, such as the building trade unions,
accomplish the same thing by establishing fixed quotas on the
number of workers who are allowed to join the union. And more
indirectly, unions often support legislation to limit foreign immigra-
tion of certain groups of people that might compete with existing
workers.

For the union, a leftward shift in labor supply does indeed
result in higher wage rates, but at the same time it reduces the
actual number of people who can enjoy that high wage. Note
Figure 6-3, in which the number of workers employed has been
reduced from L_1 to L_2. For the rest of the economy, these barriers
and restrictive policies may reduce the efficiency of the overall
economy in that individuals who want to enter are prevented from
doing so. In turn, the price of the final product to the consumer
becomes higher than if a free entry situation were in effect.

Another method of increasing wage rates is by expanding the
demand curve as shown in Figure 6-4,

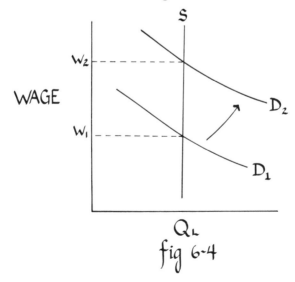

fig 6-4

How might an upward shift in the demand curve be accomplished? Recall from Chapter 4 that labor demand reflects the VMP curve. Therefore, any increase in worker productivity by adding more capital or moving up to higher states of technology will eventually shift labor demand upward. By the way, this is the major reason why wage levels in the "capital intensive" Western countries are significantly higher than the wage rates in Third World countries.

Another method of raising the demand curve would be for the union to *encourage* the purchasing of labor's final product. Why? Because the value of marginal product curve reflects not only productivity, but also the demand and the price of the final product.

Some unions assist in advertising the product while others tend to put their promotional energies indirectly into political channels. For example, construction workers often push for lower interest and mortgage rates, auto workers lobby for the construction of highways . . . or textile workers try to enlarge their own markets through the restriction of imports. These are just a few examples of how unions assist in shifting demand upward to the right.

A final method of raising wage rates involves neither a direct shift in the supply or the demand curves—but instead, reflects the sheer collective power of the union. In other words, firms may agree to a "higher than equilibrium wage rate" in order to avoid a strike. In Figure 6-5, the equilibrium wage is W_1 whereas the agreed upon wage might be as high as W_2.

The raising of wages to level W_2 appears to "defy the labor market." It looks as if the union is getting something for nothing. But alas, as with most economic benefits, there are "costs" involved. What is the drawback to this situation? Notice that in Figure 6-5 this higher wage rate intersects the labor demand curve at L_2, i.e., at a *lower* quantity of labor demanded, than the old equilibrium labor quantity of L_1. In practical terms, this means that some of the people who were formerly working would lose their job after the hike in wage rates.

On the more positive side (for the workers) it has often been asserted that *non-union* workers have frequently benefited from union wage rates in equivalent or similar industries. When such a

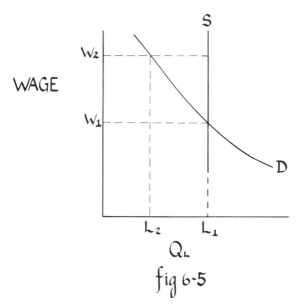

fig 6-5

situation exists, the higher non-union wage rates are usually a result of employers attempting to prevent unionization.

We could easily expand our examples of how an understanding of resource markets can enlarge our understanding of various problems and issues. But these few illustrations should be enough to give you an idea of how useful market analysis can be. Hopefully, you will be able to use this knowledge to choose a satisfying and good paying occupation for yourself.

From the topic of income distribution and resource markets, let's now turn our attention to the subject of *using product markets*—with particular emphasis on the farm problem in the United States. Why choose the agricultural industry? Because of the ease with which we can apply our knowledge of *competitive markets* as developed in Chapter 5.

You have probably heard the phrase "the farm problem." What is our "farm problem?" How did it begin, and what are some of the possible solutions? We'll carefully look at these questions and attempt to answer them in Part II of this chapter.

PART II—THE FARM PROBLEM—

Although there is no example of *perfect* competition in the United States, the agricultural industry does indeed come *closest* to our definition as we outlined it in chapter five. And in addition, our agricultural economy shares some of the great advantages and disadvantages that go along with competitive industries.

For one thing, competition is often considered a *healthy* state of affairs for the overall economy. In theory, a competitive industry will operate at peak efficiency and provide relatively low prices for the consumer. Indeed, these characteristics are beneficial to all of us.

Yet, from the viewpoint of the *producer*, the competitive agricultural industry has greatly suffered from its inability to control both output and prices—a characteristic that is particularly bad when we consider the fact that most American industries *do* have some control over *their* prices. This imbalance, in turn, has often worked to the disadvantage of the American farmer.

To see more clearly how this situation works against the farm producer, we must go back to the "root problem" of agricultural prices. Economists have, in fact, looked at the price dilemma from two vantage points—the historical price problem, and the short-run problem. Let's look first at the historical side.

The Historical Problem—

American farmers are incredible food producers. Through their exploitation of great natural resources and the intensive use of energy, farm chemicals, large-scale machinery, hybrid seeds, etc., our agricultural producers have amazed the rest of the world with both their rate of productivity and their sheer output.

One average farmer, for example, can feed himself and about *sixty* other people. Yet ironically, this amazing and enviable productivity is also the major source of our historical farm problem. Why is this so? Why does abundance have to be such a problem?

The answer can best be seen graphically. For example, our high state of farm technology has had the effect of shifting the food *supply curve* far to the right-hand side of the historical supply-demand market.

On the other hand, America's historical food *demand* has generally not kept up with the large shift in supply. Why hasn't demand kept pace? Surely the population has grown as have our incomes; but these increases have simply not matched the potential food production.

Recall that food is a product that is generally *income inelastic*. From Chapter 4 we learned that if one's income increases a certain percentage, the corresponding increase in consumption of an income-inelastic product (like food) would *not* be as great proportionately. Thus, food demand *does* increase over time—but not enough to match the large increases in supply. Nor does the population growth rate make up the difference. The ultimate result? Depressed agricultural prices relative to prices elsewhere in the economy.

A final factor compounds the overall problem—it's the fact that agricultural products are *price inelastic*; i.e., the quantities demanded are relatively insensitive to a change in price.* Inelastic demand curves, in turn, usually have a rather "steep" slope *rendering the possibility for low farm prices.* In summary, agriculture's historical problem stems from

—a large rightward shift in supply (technological advance)
—a relatively small shift in demand (income inelasticity)
—a steep demand curve (price inelasticity)

When we put all of these factors together on our historical market graph, we can easily visualize the price problem as developed over the years.

In Figure 6-6, P_1 is the equilibrium price from an earlier period. Over time, supply and demand curves shift to positions S_2 and D_2 giving a new equilibrium price of P_2 that is lower than the earlier price equilibrium.

Admittedly, Figure 6-6 is a somewhat dramatic exaggeration. The absolute prices of agricultural commodities *have not actually fallen*; what has happened, however, is that farm prices *have fallen relative* to the prices of goods that farmers pay as consumers, as well as those prices of farm inputs such as fertilizer, seed, machinery, and so forth.

This *relative* price disadvantage is sometimes referred to as a *parity problem*. A poor parity situation, for example, means that it now takes more bushels of a given commodity (for example, wheat) to purchase a given bundle of consumer goods than it did in

---

*See discussion of price elasticity in *What Is Economics?* (pp. 45-51) by Jim Eggert. © 1977 by William Kaufmann, Inc., Los Altos, California 94022.

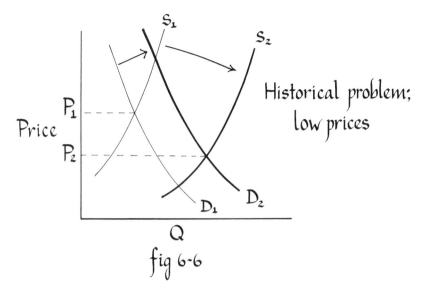

Historical problem; low prices

fig 6-6

an earlier period, say 1910-1924. To bring farmers up to some higher "level of parity" such as 90% or 100% has meant government subsidies—mainly in the form of price supports. We'll take a look at price supports and other government programs a little later. But first, let's look at the so-called "short run" agricultural problem.

The Short Run Problem—

If a deteriorating parity situation summarizes the farmers' historical problem, then their short run problem might be summarized as a year to year problem involving *the instability of farm prices, output, and income.*

Obviously, no farmer knows ahead of time what his year-end production will be—nor does he know how the industry, involving *all* suppliers, will come out in terms of production and in terms of the overall market price. There are simply too many variables; for example, lack of rain, damage from insects, fungus, or an early frost, and so on, can all reduce the supply of a given crop such as corn. Such factors may result in a high price for corn that year, but at the same time they may have left the farmer with very little to sell.

On the other hand, perfect growing conditions can result in a "bumper crop," which can be just as much of a headache as too little output. Again, we have that strange situation in which a year of plentiful food turns out to be a curse for the producers. What exactly is the problem? Perhaps it can be best explained in terms of your home garden. Has your family ever experienced an *extra good* garden crop? Perhaps some years you may have had not only twice as many beans or tomatoes as you needed, but maybe even *five times* as many. Unfortunately, everyone else is probably in the same situation at the same time, and so you can't even *give* those tomatoes away. Now imagine that your yearly income was dependent on the price of those beans or tomatoes! That will give you a feeling for the farmer's short run problem in a bumper crop year.

Figure 6-7 shows what this situation looks like for the farm industry in the short run.

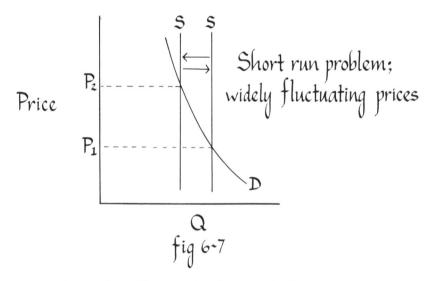

fig 6-7

Notice in the *wide variation in price* in Figure 6-7, the major causes of this situation are

—widely fluctuating supply
—inelastic demand (steep slope)

Price instability, in turn, leads to *income instability.* Even small changes in commodity prices—i.e., a few cents up or down—can have dramatic effects on the farmer's annual income. When non-farmers hear the "noon price report," they probably wonder why anyone would be interested in fractional changes in the prices of corn or wheat or hogs...or any other commodity. Yet, these small changes can easily make the difference between profit and loss for the average farm producer. Few industries face an equivalent situation of income uncertainty on a year to year basis.

Our discussion of the two related farm problems leads us to an important question: What (if anything) can be done about them?

Unfortunately, no one has yet discovered a sure-fire, low-cost solution for either the historical or the short run problem. There have been various government efforts to help the American farmer; looking at these efforts with the aid of our product markets, we'll be able to "see" the advantages as well as the disadvantages of the governmental programs.

Government Farm Programs—

Let's look first at the government's *crop restriction* (sometimes called the "soil bank") program. Once it is recognized that much of the farm problem stems from a situation of over-supply, it is easy to see the logic of restricting the number of acres that farmers are allowed to plant.

In essence, the crop restriction program pays the farmer to keep a certain amount of his land out of production. If we look at this situation on our market graph, crop restriction has the effect of shifting the supply curve backwards (i.e., to the left) and also brings about *higher* agriculture prices, as Figure 6-8 indicates.

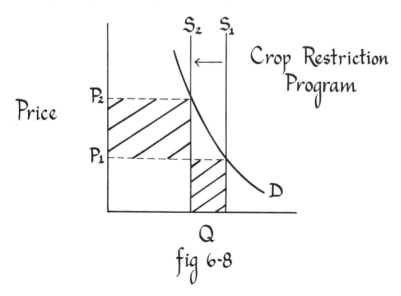

fig 6-8

Besides receiving a higher price for the farm commodity (P_2), the farmer would also gain a *higher total revenue* for producing *less* output. But how do we know this for a fact? Note that in Figure 6-8 the total revenue lost (as represented by the smaller shaded rectangle) is smaller than the total revenue gained (the larger shaded rectangle). This will always be true—i.e., a higher price leading to greater total revenue—whenever we are dealing with an inelastic demand curve. In summary, the farmer's benefits from crop restrictions are

—extra money from the government for keeping his land out of production
—high commodity prices and greater total revenue

Yet, this program has some major drawbacks for taxpayers, as well as for the general consumer. These disadvantages would include

—higher taxes to support the crop restriction program
—higher prices to consumers and less food available for consumption

In another form of intervention, the *price support program*, the government tries to deal more directly with the "price and income instability" problems. Basically, this program does two positive things for the farm; it *increases and stabilizes* commodity prices above the normal equilibrium price. The price support program's effects are shown graphically in Figure 6-9.

In Figure 6-9, the government's support price is P_s, a price well above the original equilibrium price. This higher price will give the farmer a greater total revenue because of the inelasticity of the demand curve. However, the higher support price has also had the effect of *cutting back the quantity demanded* (i.e., from Q_1 to Q_2). Yet, supply will remain constant at the original level. The inevitable result of this situation is that a *surplus is created* which must be bought up by the government at the support price. The quantity of this surplus is the difference between Q_1 and Q_2, and the cost of buying up the surplus is represented by the shaded area. When the government buys up this surplus, it is a bonus income for the farmers, to be sure, but it is also a headache for taxpayers. Along with the cost of buying up the surpluses, taxpayers face an addi-

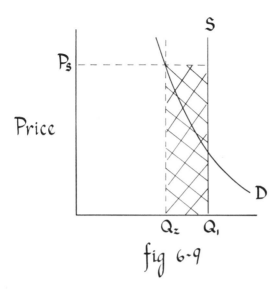

fig 6-9

tional expense of storing the surplus. And, as before, the consumer winds up with higher food prices.

So, there is not a simple solution to either the historical or the short run problem. In recent years, the government has moved to limit both the crop restriction programs, and also the price support subsidies. Government help, however, is coming in on the *demand* side. Specifically, our large Food Stamp program plus a greater emphasis on food *exports* has had the effect of shifting the demand curve to the right. These programs, in turn, help both the farmer and the consumer—particularly low income consumers.

At this point, we cannot claim that agriculture's deep-seated problems have by any means been solved. But at least we *can* say that, through our work in developing a competitive market, we have a great advantage in *understanding* the farm problem, as well as being able to see the strengths and shortcomings of the major farm programs of our federal government.

Chapter 7
Background to the Long Run

Until now, our discussions of competitive supply have been primarily concerned with the *short run*. I'm sure you remember our earlier example for describing Chester's diminishing return situation. The condition was that he keep all his resources fixed except for the one variable resource of labor. And it was out of this strict short run condition that we derived Chester's upward sloping competitive supply curve.

But what would happen if we suddenly dropped this strict condition? What if we allow Chester the opportunity to expand or contract the amount of land he farms, or to add more capital...or to alter any other resource? If we allow Chester this kind of freedom, we shall be in what economists call *the long run*. The long run, in this sense, is a "new ball game," and it involves a different approach from our earlier short run approach.

Let's examine this new situation then, using our old friend Chester Olson as our representative of a typical competitive producer.

Long Run Defined—

I personally find it easiest to remember what the long run is all about by thinking of it as a time period that is long enough so that *all resources become variable resources*. In the short run, Chester could not get out of paying for things like land costs, insurance, depreciation, taxes, and so forth. But in the "long run" time period, we are assuming he can reduce or expand any resource that formerly was fixed.

Thus, at the one extreme, the long run allows a producer the opportunity to leave farming altogether (if he cannot meet his economic costs), and at the other extreme, it means he has the opportunity to purchase entire new farms—to double or triple the scale of his operation if that's what he wants to do. Economists use the term *scale of operation* to indicate that the producer can now enlarge or reduce *all resources.*

Is it possible to show the "long run" by means of a graphical approach? Fortunately we have at our disposal a technique of showing "scale changes" that will greatly aid us in our research of the long run. It is a technique, in fact, that is surprisingly similar to the *indifference curve-budget line* system that we developed back in Chapter 2. This new technique is called the *equal-product curve-budget line system.* The similarities between these two systems will be pointed out as we move along.

The Equal Product Curve—

Note that Figure 7-1 shows a curve that looks very much like our earlier indifference curve. This time, however, instead of two "goods" on the x and y axes (our "hamburgers" and "milkshakes"), we have two different resources: capital (K) and labor (L). And instead of having a curve that shows "a constant

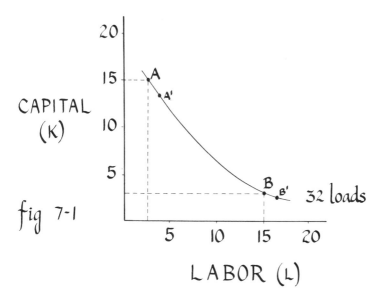

fig 7-1

level of utility," this new curve will show *a constant level of output.* That is why this curve is called "an equal product curve".

Recall that Chester Olson is now in the long run, and assume that this first equal product curve shown in Figure 7-1 represents an output of 32 loads of hay per day.

An equal product curve such as this shows us *all the combinations of capital (K) and labor (L)* that would generate 32 loads of hay. For example, at point A, the combination of 15 units of K and about 2 units of L will give Chester 32 loads . . . but so will point B, which represents 15 units of L and about 3 of K, . . . and so will any points in between A and B generate exactly the same output!

Notice that Chester's equal product curve is shaped very much like our old indifference curve from the theory of demand; both are "convex" to the origin. What does this mean in relation to an equal product curve? It means that if Chester wants to maintain 32 loads of hay and move from point A to A', he would have to give up quite a bit of capital to do this. On the other hand, if he is at point B and wishes to move to the more "labor-intensive" situation of B', the necessary reduction in capital would not have to be so great as before. Thus, this apparent "falling substitutability of capital for labor" would give rise to a curve that shows a *falling slope* as Chester moves generally from A to B (or to a more labor-intensive method of producing hay). This falling slope can be seen graphically in Figure 7-2.

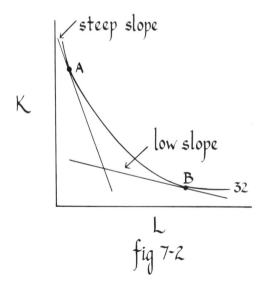

fig 7-2

We can make other comparisons, too, between indifference and equal product curves. For example, Chester has the opportunity, in the long run, to move onto higher and higher equal product curves, just as the consumer could move onto higher indifference curves. Each new equal product curve that moves upward to the right will represent higher levels of output. When a number of curves are placed together on one graph, we have a production *map* or what is more commonly referred to as a *production function*. A production function will show the thousands and thousands of resource combinations that will produce any given level of output. Figure 7-3 shows a partial production function with 3 possible levels of output. One might, of course, enlarge the graph and draw in other possible levels as well.

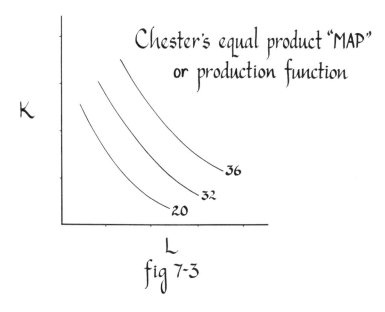

Chester's equal product "MAP"
or production function

fig 7-3

Another comparison with indifference analysis is the existence of a *budget line*. The budget line in Chester's example represents a certain budget to pay for production costs. The producer's budget line is drawn in exactly the same fashion as we drew the consumer's budget line back in Chapter 2. You may wish to read again our earlier explanation (pages 19-20) if you feel uneasy about how these lines are derived.

Once the budget line has been drawn for any given level of budget, we are able to "see" exactly where Chester *maximizes* his output within a given budget . . . just as the consumer maximized utility with his budget. Of course, when we say Chester is maximizing output with a given budget, we are also saying that "he is minimizing his costs" in producing that many loads of hay.

Let's now assume that Chester is given the opportunity to spend a fixed amount, say $300, and then see how he maximizes his output on that fixed budget. In Figure 7-4 the budget line represents $300.

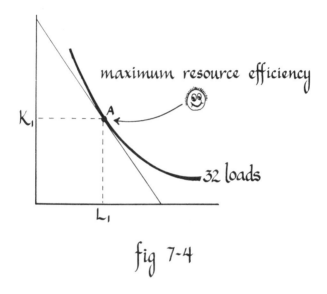

fig 7-4

The point of maximum efficiency is really no surprise. It's the same kind of "solution" we obtained at the end of Chapter 2, but now the producer maximizes output (or minimizes costs) at the point where the equal-product curve is tangent to the budget line. In Figure 7-4, that "optimal" point is obviously point A. Once we have found the tangency, we can "dot" over to the K (capital) axis, and then down to the L (labor) axis to find out the "best" or most efficient combination of resources Chester can use to produce the 32 loads of hay. The ideal resource mix would therefore be K_1 and L_1.

One reason we are taking pains to make all these comparisons between the theory of demand and the theory of production is to show the amazing similarities between consumer behavior and producer behavior. They are both trying to maximize their individual objectives under financial constraints. The producer attempts to maximize *output,* while the consumer tries to maximize *utility* with his limited budget.

The major difference between producer and consumer theory, however, is that Chester Olson as a producer is not just after an efficient use of resources; he also wants to maximize his *profits* as well. Profit maximization, in turn, makes our discussion of supply comparatively more complex than of demand, and hence will it take more time.

Chester Goes to India—

Let's again return to Chester's efficiency position as seen in Figure 7-4. Now, just for fun, we will try an experiment. Let's transfer our hay-baling friend to a "labor intensive, capital poor" country such as India.

India has an extremely large labor supply which contributes to a situation of depressed wages (like the "waitress market" of Chapter 6). On the other hand, India's capital shortage means relatively high capital prices compared to the United States. These resource prices, in turn, will *force* Chester into a different pattern of production. We can see how this works using the equal product curve approach.

The first thing we must realize is that equal product curves in India will look *just like* equal product curves in the U.S. The "mix" of resources that can produce a certain level of output is more or less a "mechanical arrangement", where so much input anywhere in the world will result in the same output. So what is the major difference between India and the U.S.?

Graphically, the major difference between countries would be the *slope of the budget line.* For example, a $300 budget in India could obviously buy a great deal of labor because of India's relatively low labor costs. However, in that same country, Chester *would not be able* to buy much capital because of capital's high cost.

The resulting budget line for India would come out looking like an extremely low sloped line. Figure 7-5 shows a budget line comparison between the U.S. and India. Note that there is a relatively steep sloped budget line for the U.S. because of our *high cost of labor* and relatively *low cost of capital*.

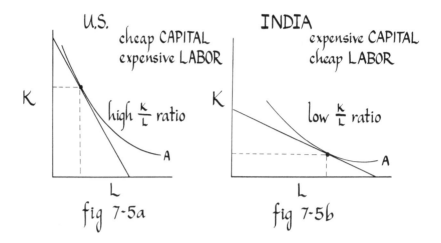

fig 7-5a   fig 7-5b

What is so interesting about these two diagrams is that they clearly show the dramatic impact that *different resource prices* have upon the way a country will produce its products. For example, "production efficiency" in the U.S. is defined by a resource mix that represents a *high capital to labor ratio* (i.e., a high K/L ratio). Indeed, this is really no surprise as we frequently see businesses using more capital intensive methods as labor costs become higher and higher.

But "efficiency" in India is just the reverse, and there Chester will produce the maximum output in India with a very *low* K/L ratio; i.e., a very *labor intensive* technique. One might jump to the conclusion that just because India winds up with a labor intensive method of producing hay, its system is necessarily less efficient that the United States capital intensive system. However, this conclusion may not be correct. To find out which country's production method is more efficient, we would have to compare the *overall* costs of production. If we assume that Chester is operating on the same budget and producing the same output, then the two countries would be *equally* efficient. What this situation really demonstrates is that each country has its own unique set of resource prices which determine its most "efficient" methods of production.

The Expansion Line —

Let's bring Chester Olson back to his original farm in America and offer him what we originally promised him—the chance to use a wide variety of budgets, plus the "long run" freedom to change *any or all* of his resources. Then we can watch him expand his scale of operation while we note down the points of tangency between equal product curves and the new budget lines. We will then connect the points of tangency with a line that economists call *the expansion line*. The expansion line, in turn, will show Chester precisely which combinations of capital and labor will most efficiently produce a large variety of output levels. Figure 7-6 illustrates a simple expansion line utilizing 5 equal product curves.

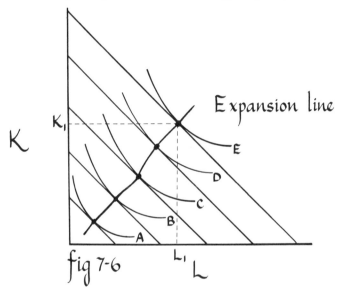

fig 7-6

With the expansion line, it is possible for Chester to choose any level of output, then find the point of tangency and "dot" over to the x and y axis to find out the "best" combination of capital and labor. For example, at output level E in Figure 7-6, Chester would find that L_1 and K_1 would turn out to be the most efficient resource mix. From the expansion line, we can also see how our present "long run" situation differs from the short run conditions of previous chapters. Note how Chester is changing *both* capital and labor, whereas before, he was not allowed to change the level of capital.

Long Run Average Cost—

We are now in a good position to discuss what is perhaps the most important idea of this chapter—the derivation of Chester's *long run average cost curve.* You might be wondering why we are so interested in discussing "one more" cost concept. After all, did we not spend a lot of time and energy developing the *marginal cost* concept which was also important?

Indeed, marginal cost is *still* a crucial concept as it helps us determine where a producer will *maximize his profits.* The long run average cost curve, on the other hand, will be our best measure of *output efficiency.* But again you are probably wondering, "Didn't we already analyze the idea of *efficiency* when we discussed the point of tangency above?" Yes, we did discuss efficiency—but it was only *one kind of efficiency,* i.e., the best combination or "mix" of resources in which to produce an A, B, C, D, or E level of output.

But what we do not yet know is, which of the different *levels* of output is the optimum level? For example, level A may be only one load of hay per day (see Figure 7-6). Sure, we now know the "best" combination of resources to produce this 1 load. But there may well be certain "efficiencies of size" if we go to some higher level of output, because large-scale businesses can often produce more cheaply than small-scale operations. These size efficiencies are referred to as "economies of scale". Which level of output (A, B, C, D or E) will maximize these economies of scale? We can find out by calculating which level of output will give Chester's lowest average cost. How would Chester figure these average costs?

Fortunately, it's not too difficult once we have a few figures from our equal product curve graph. For simplicity's sake, we'll assume that a unit of labor is worth $20 and a unit of capital is also worth $20.

We can now help Chester decide upon his first budget. To start off, let's give him $100. At $20 per unit for labor, the maximum potential labor quantity with this budget would be 5 units. Thus, the budget line would strike the labor axis at the 5 unit level. On the other hand, if Chester spent all of his $100 on capital and none on labor, he could buy 5 units of capital. This budget line is shown as the smallest budget in Figure 7-7.

Next, we will give Chester $200, and work out a budget line for that amount. Then we will give him $300, $400, and finally $500. Each new and higher budget is represented by an expanding budget line in Figure 7-7.

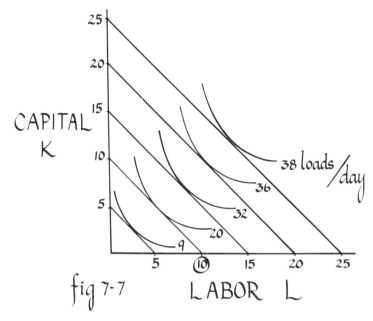

fig 7-7   LABOR L

Finally, we will draw the relevant *equal product curve* which is tangent to each of these budget lines, and note the output that is associated with each equal product curve. From these figures, in turn, we can derive our long run average costs.

Let's work an example, using the information in Figure 7-7. Look carefully at the budget line which strikes the labor axis at 10 units (note that the number 10 on the labor axis is circled). Remembering that labor is priced at $20, we know that this particular budget must be worth $200 (i.e., 10 x $20 = $200). Next, we read off the maximum output that is possible for this $200 budget as represented by the equal product curve that is tangent to this budget line (it's worth 20 loads of hay, right?).

Thus, the average cost of producing hay is:

$200/20 loads = $10 per load (average cost)

Therefore, the average cost of producing 20 loads of hay would be $10 per load. Using the same method, we can easily go on to figure out the average costs at the other points of tangency as well. And each time we get an average cost in relation to a certain quantity, we have a new point which we can graph on Chester's long run average cost curve. Rounding off to the nearest half-dollar, we get the following average costs:

$$\frac{Budget}{loads} = LAC$$

① $\frac{\$100}{9\ loads} = \$11/load$

② $\frac{\$200}{20\ loads} = \$10/load$

③ $\frac{\$300}{32\ loads} = \$9\frac{1}{2}/load$

④ $\frac{\$400}{36\ loads} = \$11/load$

⑤ $\frac{\$500}{38\ loads} = \$13/load$

And, finally, using the above data, we're able to graph five points on the *long run average cost curve* which, from now on, will be abbreviated as "the LAC curve."

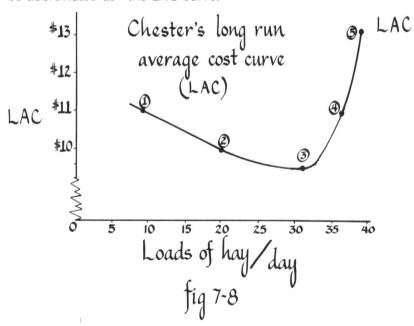

Chester's long run average cost curve (LAC)

Loads of hay/day

fig 7-8

The above LAC curve has an interesting shape to it, which raises some questions. Why, for example, do you think it first turns down, and then at about 32 loads (point 3), begins to turn up again? What do you think is the "optimal" level of output? How does this curve relate to the process of profit maximization? We will be taking a close look at these and other interesting questions as we move on to Chapter 8, a chapter devoted to deriving and discussing the long run competitive supply curve.

Chapter 8

Long Run Supply

In Chapter 7, we derived Chester Olson's long run average cost curve (LAC) from a system of equal product curves. Now we are going to spend some time discussing the *shape* of the LAC curve, which represents another part of our continuing quest to understand the nature of *economic efficiency*.

A little later on, we will look at the question, "How does Chester maximize his profits in the long run?" Our answer to this question will lead us to consider *the long run competitive supply curve.*

And finally, we will try to connect the concepts of "efficiency" and "profits" together within the context of a competitive market structure.

To begin our discussion, it will be helpful to look back at Chester's LAC curve in Figure 7-8. Note its "U"-like shape. It is certainly not a symetrical U, but the curve does drop steadily to 32 loads of hay, and after that, it rises fairly sharply.

What is the reason for the U shape? Are we once again experiencing a situation of increasing returns, and then diminishing returns? No, not this time. Recall that diminishing returns always involved a *fixed* resource situation. But now Chester is "in the long run", a time period in which he can vary all his resources.

So what causes this drop and rise of LAC? The answer is the phenomenon introduced in Chapter 7 that we call "economies of scale". Closely related to the idea of "economies of scale" is the idea of "diseconomies of scale." Let's now take a close look at these interesting ideas.

Economies & Diseconomies of Scale —

Returning once again to Chester's hay baling operation, we see that when he produces only 9 loads a day, his average cost per load is $11. As he expands his operation, however, he is able to reduce average costs. They drop to a low of $9½ dollars per load as his scale moves up to 32 loads per day. As we noted in Chapter 7, this drop in average cost is caused by the "economies of scale" of baling hay. What are these mysterious *economies of scale?*

Economies of scale are simply various cost cutting efficiencies that can be introduced in some industries as the scale of operation grows. Certainly the most common "economy of scale" is a result of *specialization and division of labor.* There are also efficiencies to be gained through the use of *larger and more productive machinery.*

Let's look at "specialization" a little closer. When workers specialize, they can usually learn to do their specific jobs quicker and more accurately than one worker can who shifts around from job to job (as, for example, Chester did when he was baling by himself). With the larger scale of operation, more people, more tractors, more wagons, etc., one man can specialize in loading hay, another in driving the tractor with the baler, another in taking loads back and forth, another in unloading, and so on. After a while, Chester's baling crew will be able to operate like an "assembly-line" operation because of this specialization.

Also, consider the possibilities for larger machinery. A baler that costs $1,000 might easily be *more than twice* as productive as a $500 machine. You can see these economies of scale at work on many large farms, with their huge tractors, plows, and other machinery.

Economies of scale can also be observed in other industries. For example, if someone tried to produce automobiles on a scale of 100 cars per year, their average cost per car would obviously be extremely high; but, if they are able to "up the scale" to 30,000 cars per year, they will find thousands of both big and little efficiencies that work to bring average costs down.

In addition, large businesses often operate dozens of separate *plants* which are able to take advantage of specialized expertise at the management levels, as well as efficiencies of purchasing large quantities versus small quantities. Good examples of such businesses are the McDonald's restaurants and K-Mart retail stores, where we see economies passed on to the consumer in the form of relatively low prices. Indeed, from Henry Ford's original assembly line to large-scale farming to McDonald's hamburgers, the average consumer has benefited from production techniques based on *bigness*.

Yet, we should also recognize some drawbacks as well. Large-scale concerns often take on an "impersonal dimension" for both the employees and for their customers. In addition, workers on the bottom may frequently suffer from chronic *boredom* which extreme specialization may produce. Indeed, the long run average cost curve of a business may continue to fall as the organization gets larger and more specialized but keep in mind that the LAC curve represents *monetary costs* only.

If it were possible to have some simple measurement (like "dollars") for the *psychic costs*, we might find that organizations reach their "optimal" efficiency long before the average monetary costs reach their optimum. Figure 8-1 illustrates a possible situation which compares *average economic costs* with *average psychic costs* for a sample large-scale system. The organization might be a business, a factory, a government agency, or even a hospital, a school, or a city.

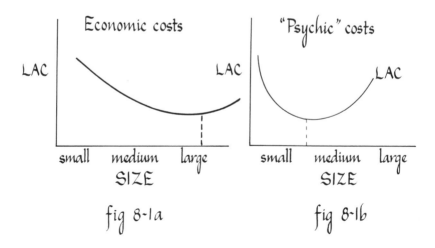

fig 8-1a   fig 8-1b

If the comparisons shown in Figure 8-1 are in fact true, we can assume that as the system gets larger, its average economic costs drop, and it would be cheaper to build a car, to treat a hospital patient, to educate a child, or to administer a city. But if the psychic cost curve is accurate, psychological diseconomies set in far earlier.* Indeed, this would be an excellent issue for further study from a variety of viewpoints including psychological and sociological, as well as economic.

Yet, even without the problem of "psychic costs," long run average monetary *cost* curves eventually *will* turn upward on their own. In Chester's hay baling example, his LAC curve began to rise after approximately 32 loads of hay. In Figure 8-1, the LAC curve begins to rise after a certain large scale has been reached. What's happening now?

When LAC starts to rise, the production system has reached a point where *the diseconomies of scale* tend to outweigh the economies of scale. Sometimes it's interesting to try to imagine *what* these diseconomies might be for different productive organizations, and at what point the diseconomies will be greater than the economies of scale. Let's take a look at some examples.

In Chester's case, diseconomies probably begin to emerge when he finds himself wasting time and fuel as he hauls his tractors and machinery around his enlarged farm operation. Another diseconomy becomes apparent as he discovers a growing difficulty in *coordinating* all the separate and diverse factors (people, machines, etc.) that must be accurately synchronized to maintain efficient production. Related to this problem is the increasing difficulty of gaining accurate information as the size of the farm's operation increases; and without a good knowledge of what is going on, Chester finds himself making decisions based on inadequate information—decisions which wind up costing him money. In addition, his large machinery may mean more costly repair work, and "one sunny day's breakdown" will become far more expensive to him than it was with a smaller operation. There are probably many other special reasons why Chester's kind of

---

*For support of this thesis and further discussion of the disadvantages of bigness, see *Small Is Beautiful* by E. F. Schumacher, © 1973, Harper and Row, and also the writings of another British economist, Ezra Mishan.

production system tends to get more costly after a certain point, but now, let's take a look at some other situations.

For large businesses, diseconomies frequently crop up in the form of *bureaucratic red tape,* or of trying to get things done through layers and layers of hierarchical decision making. And just as in Chester's case, upper level management people in large businesses often have difficulty in knowing what is going on at the lower levels. Some organizations are simply too big, too spread out. And in order to try to get information, middle and upper level management people find themselves spending more and more time in meetings and conferences. They also need to know the opinions of a growing army of management specialists. Yet, these hour to hour sessions of highly paid executives in big companies take their toll in costs. Smaller companies on the other hand, can often avoid these kinds of diseconomies.

Larger companies may also be more rigid on certain kinds of policies such as approving new ideas or hiring particularly gifted men and women. There are also other kinds of diseconomies. Perhaps you can think of some types of jobs that relate specifically to larger companies—jobs that would probably not exist if the organization were smaller. (Possible examples would be security personnel, parking lot attendents, legal and public relations departments—just to name a few.) You may find it interesting to check the personnel directory of a very large corporation or institution and note down the kinds of jobs which probably would not exist if the organization were smaller.

Of course, these are often little diseconomies—but they do add up. At some point, they begin to outweigh the more commonly known economies of scale. And when this finally does happen, the long run average cost curves begin to rise.

Double Efficiency—

It is now time to summarize and tie together what we have learned about the important subject of "economic efficiency."

Returning once again to our friend Chester Olson, we have just found out that he will experience economies of scale as he enlarges his operation up to a certain point—32 loads of hay per day. And it is *only* at that quantity that he can produce hay for the *lowest possible average cost* of $9½ dollars per load. Thus, 32 loads is that special scale of output where Chester's economies are in full force. In fact, it would also be the "correct" capacity for *any* producer who is using the same level of baling technology as Chester.

We therefore have one kind of efficiency—*the efficiency of scale*—that is represented by the *bottom point* on a long run average cost curve.

What we tend to forget, however, is that this low point on the LAC curve also represents the other kind of efficiency too—i.e., *the right mix of resources*. This kind of efficiency, in turn, is represented by the *tangency* of the equal product curve with its respective budget line.

Thus, there is a kind of *double efficiency* that takes place at the bottom of the long run average cost curve. In Figure 8-2, we have combined these two efficiency ideas in order to see how the two systems relate to each other.

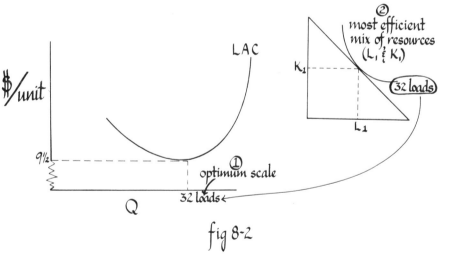

fig 8-2

To summarize, the 32 load level of output and the $9½ average represents a point of "double efficiency" because

—it's an optimum output or scale (considering all outputs)
—it's the most efficient mix of resources (for that output)

Now if the double efficiency point on Chester's LAC curve is such an "ideal" situation from the economic point of view, will Chester, in fact, actually operate there? In other words, Chester *should* produce at the 32 load level, but will he?

Before we can answer that question, we've got to find out how he will go about *maximizing his profits*. For only if the two are equal—i.e., the point of efficiency is the same point of profit maximization—can we be sure that our competitive model works to promote economic efficiency. Let's go find out.

Efficiency and Profits—

Perhaps the most logical question to begin with is, "Is there a good method of predicting at what point Chester will maximize profits?" Fortunately, we have already worked out a technique of determining profit maximization. Recall from Chapter 5 that Chester will always add to his output as long as the long run marginal cost (LMC) is *less* than the price of a load of hay. If he can make even a tiny profit on an extra load of hay, he should continue to produce hay. It is only when the extra costs exceed the value of a load of hay that he knows he must stop adding to his output. We concluded in Chapter 5 that Chester will have reached the maximum profit position when the *marginal cost equaled the price.*

Fortunately, nothing has changed this theory—even though we are now in a long run situation. We do have one problem, however; we have not yet worked out what Chester's *long run marginal costs* look like. Our only long run information is summarized by the LAC curve that we developed earlier. Without knowing *long run marginal costs* we would have no way of figuring out profitability.

Is it possible to approximate his marginal costs by using his LAC curve? Again the answer is "yes". Indeed, the relationship between marginal and average costs is well worth looking into.

The Relationship Between Marginal and Average Costs—

One of the best methods of seeing how "marginal" and "average" relate to each other is to look at a topic of far more immediate concern to students—their *grade point averages.* We shall return to the subject of cost comparisons in a moment.

The secret to connecting average with marginal is to recognize that one's grade point average is made up of many, many marginal grades. In fact, it's the "marginals" that increase or lower an average.

For example, let's assume that you get an "A" in economics, but your overall average grade for all of your courses is a "C." The A is your "marginal grade"; that is, it is the extra grade you get from taking an extra course. Now if your marginal grade is *above* your overall average, it will have the effect of *pulling the average up*. Of course, that marginal A will not lift your overall average to an A, but it will pull it up a little bit.

On the other hand, if your "marginal" grade were a "D", it would obviously pull the overall average down.

Now let's return to the world of economic costs. If the above analogy holds, we will know that if the average (i.e., the LAC curve) is falling, it *must* mean that the marginal cost is *below* it. That is, very low marginal costs pull average cost down just as very low marginal grades pull one's average grade point down.

On the other hand, if LAC is moving upward, then we can be certain that marginal costs must be *above* LAC (just as your A grades pull up your average).

One important characteristic of this relationship is that *the instant LMC is a fraction of a dollar above LAC, it starts pulling LAC up*. This, in turn, means that LMC strikes through LAC at the very bottom of the LAC curve; i.e., at *the most efficient scale of output*.

We can easily see this unique relationship in Figure 8-3.

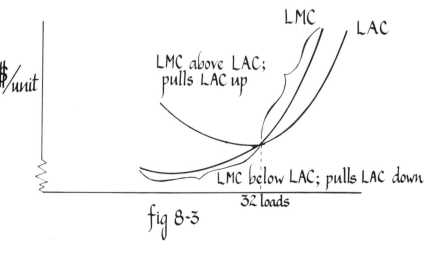

fig 8-3

The very fact that LMC, which is *the* guideline to maximum profitability happens to be exactly equivalent to LAC at *its* most desirable point, is indeed a good omen.

But alas, there are also many other points on Chester's LMC profitability curve as well. If the price of a load of hay happens to be above the $9½ level, or below it, then Chester will maximize profits at some "non-optimum" point. What we need is some kind of "guarantee" that the overall industry price of hay will settle at the $9½ level. Then Chester will equate price with his long run marginal costs at that point that also coincides with the bottom of his LAC curve.

Is there any unique characteristic of the competitive market model that will guarantee this "correct" price? Once again, we can answer in the affirmative! The key competitive attribute is *easy entry, easy exit.*

The fact that small competitors can easily enter or leave the industry *will* guarantee the $9½ price, because only at that price will there be no excessive long run profits. Let's take an example.

Suppose the price in the short run were $12, a price that would give hay producers a *temporary profit* because it would be greater than average costs. This profit will be a "signal" for a swarm of small producers to move in (remember the hog example in Chapter 5?) to increase overall supply which will have the effect of driving the price back down to the only "no profit" price of $9½ where price equals average cost.

Perhaps you are objecting to the fact that Chester is going to wind up at a *break-even situation* in the long run, even though he is pursuing a policy of "maximum profits." Keep in mind, however, that we assume that *all* of Chester's economic costs are being met (i.e., explicit, implicit, and social costs).

Thus, a "no profit" situation still means that Chester is paying himself a fair wage and he is also earning a decent rate of return on his investment. But outside of these economic returns, Chester *has virtually no control* over the tendency for other hay producers to move in, if and when the price of hay goes above average costs. Indeed, in the short run, there might be extra profits because, by definition, the short run is not a long enough period for producers to move in and out. But in the long run, we must assume they can move in, and if the price is right, they will.

This situation will operate in reverse too. For example, if the price should happen to dip *below* the $9½ level, it means that there will be some losses within the industry, as the price would be lower than average cost.

But again, the long run is a long enough period of time so that some of the loss operations can move out of the industry altogether. This will have the effect of cutting back the overall industry supply and eventually raising the industry price back up to the $9½ level.

What is important to see now is how the "easy entry, easy exit" characteristic of the competitive market model *forces the suppliers to operate where we want them to;* i.e., at that quantity where the LAC curve is lowest and the maximum economies of scale are in effect.

Therefore, in the long run, we have a rather "strange" looking supply curve for a *perfectly competitive industry.* It is basically a *horizontal line* (Figure 8-4b) emanating from the y axis at the very lowest possible long run average cost. Of course, the possibility exists that, if industry output gets "too" large, it may take more money to attract additional resources; and if basic industry costs rise, we would expect an eventual upward turn in the long run supply curve. This situation is represented by the dotted line in Figure 8-4b.

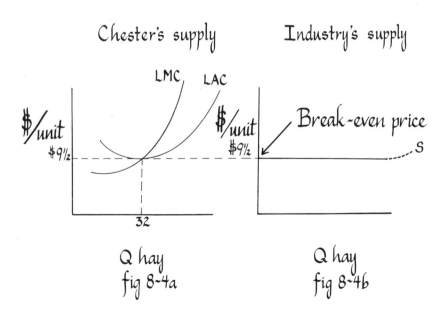

Chester's supply

Industry's supply

LMC LAC

$/unit

$9½

32

Q hay

fig 8-4a

$/unit

$9½

Break-even price

S

Q hay

fig 8-4b

In conclusion, we can say that purely competitive industries will supply as much output as is needed, and at the lowest possible cost (in the long run)—a truly remarkable conclusion! And bear in mind that this means that not only is our ong run competitive solution "good" for the economy in terms of economic efficiency, but also that it is a solution that offers the *consumer* a product for a price that is equal to the lowest average cost possible. These are the major reasons why economists find the competitive model so attractive.

Competition and Monopoly—

Farming happens to be a good example of competition partly because its ideal scale is *relatively small* compared with the overall demand for the product. This means that agriculture, as an industry, can apparently accommodate thousands and thousands of small, efficient operators. Thus, by just looking at the scale requirements of farming compared with the demand curve, one should be able to predict that this industry would be an ideal setting for competition. We can "see" one example of this situation depicted in Figure 8-5. (Be sure to note the change in the x axis from 32 loads to 320,000 loads.)

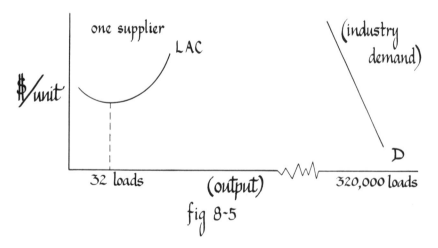

fig 8-5

But what would happen if another kind of industry *needs* a large scale of operation to take advantage of all the scale efficiencies—but there is not sufficient demand to make the industry competitive? An extreme example of this situation is the electrical utility industry, where the demand might not be sufficient to meet the most efficient scale requirements. We have graphed this situation in Figure 8-6.

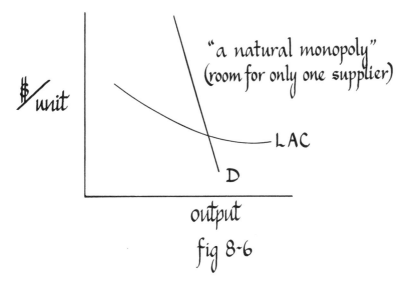

"a natural monopoly"
(room for only one supplier)

LAC

D

output

fig 8-6

Note that in this example, we have a continually dropping LAC curve. Apparently, there is room for *only one* producer in this market. It is obviously a situation that is precisely the opposite from our competitive model. What we have, of course, is an environment that is made to order for a *monopolist*. This particular extreme situation would be considered a "natural monopoly" since even one more supplier would be economically unnecessary. Natural and other kinds of monopolies, in turn, raise some very important questions—i.e., how do they operate in regards to pricing and efficiency? How do they stack up against the competitive market structure? Are monopolies "good" or "bad" for the overall economy? These and other questions will be examined as we zero in on the monopoly market structure in the next chapter.

Chapter 9

Monopoly

Before we say much about "monopoly", we should say something about "imperfect competition". As you probably know, most of the industries in the U.S. are not really "competitive" if we match them up against our strict competitive market definition. As we noted at the end of Chapter 8, some industries, such as an electrical utility or a telephone service, *need* such a large scale of operation that there is only room for about *one* seller. Other industries, such as auto, steel, or television manufacture, also need large scale operation. Generally speaking, they can accommodate a number of firms, but not the "thousands and thousands" needed to be called "a competitive market."

In addition to scale requirement, we also find situations where "the competition" is actively *discouraged by the existing firms.* They may erect artificial barriers such as patent protection, monopolization of raw materials, brand name recognition, and sometimes aggressive price cutting—all in order to discourage rivals from entering the industry.

Thus, with a variety of entry barriers, we have a "real world" economic environment that has different market structures in addition to the purely competitive market structure. These *imperfect, or non-competitive* markets range from the pure monopolist down to a model called differentiated competition. You can see how these different markets relate to each other in Figure 9-1. They are listed according to their level of concentration.

Thus, if we are going to get a more accurate picture of how our economy actually works, we must go beyond the competitive

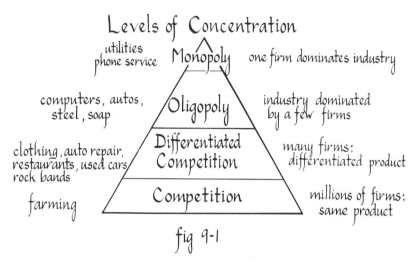

Levels of Concentration

utilities, phone service — Monopoly — one firm dominates industry

computers, autos, steel, soap — Oligopoly — industry dominated by a few firms

clothing, auto repair, restaurants, used cars, rock bands — Differentiated Competition — many firms; differentiated product

farming — Competition — millions of firms; same product

fig 9-1

market structure—the model on which we have already spent most of our time and energy. Well, does this mean that we must start from scratch, that we must begin all over again with resource pricing, deriving cost curves, etc.? Fortunately, no. Our production theory for non-competitive systems is nearly the same, as *all firms* will have similar LAC and LMC curves based on their production functions. So, what is the difference between the competitive and the three non-competitive market structures?

The major difference between these markets is *the quality and the shape of an individual firm's demand curve*. This demand curve, in turn, will be based upon the firm's control over the total market. For example, the monopolist has the entire industry demand all to himself. We'll be looking at this situation in some detail in this chapter.

The oligopoly and differentiated-competition market structures have their unique demand situations that reflect their respective ability to control the market. We will be taking a look at these two models in the next chapter. But for now, let's turn our attention to the monopolies to see what makes them "tick."

Monopoly Defined—

It is easiest to remember a monopoly market as a *one-firm industry*. In theory, there are absolutely *no substitutes* to the monopolist's product. The consumer, therefore, has virtually no choice—either you buy from him, or you don't buy. As we learned at the end of Chapter 8, the monopolist might attain his special status by scale requirements alone—i.e., the market cannot logically contain more than one seller (such as an electric utility). If this is the case, it's usually called a *natural monopoly*.

On the other hand, there have also been cases (such as the formation of the original Standard Oil Company), where the monopoly attained its dominant position by ruthless price-cutting practices in order to "freeze out" the competition. Economists would call a firm in this situation a *predatory monopolist*.

Monopolies can also be formed through revolutionary technology or through the control of raw materials—and other techniques as well. Yet, however it is formed, the monopolist winds up with the entire *industry demand* all to himself. Of course, there are *some* limits to the monopolist's power.

For example, even though a monopolist controls prices, he must still operate within the confines and constraints of the industry demand. Thus, if he decides to charge some outrageous price, the monopolist will discover (as with any other business) that nobody will turn up to buy the product.

Nevertheless, price control *does* work to the monopolist's advantage in that he is able to "fine-tune" the industry price to gain a maximum amount of monopoly profits. Certainly no other market structure enjoys so much control over price.

To show how a pure monopolist uses price control to maximize profits, let's make up a new example. Can we pretend for a minute that Chester Olson, now fed up with the risks and uncertainties of producing and baling hay, decides to become a manufacturer of hay-baling equipment? And let's further pretend that over a long period of painstaking research, our friend comes up with a new, improved *revolutionary* kind of hay-baling machine.

The John Deere and International Harvestor companies are shocked to discover that this simple farmer has invented a low-cost baler that is so efficient, it makes all other balers virtually obsolete. Articles appear in all the farm trade journals praising Chester as "the new Henry Ford" of hay balers. And despite some start-up problems, Chester establishes a huge baler factory and successfully markets his baler nationally.

As an effective monopolist, Chester now finds himself in a much different and much more favorable position than when he was just plain "Chester Olson, competitive hay-supplier." In the old days, he had to abide by the industry price, no matter what it was.

Now Chester can set his own price in order to gain a maximum profit within the constraints of market demand and costs of production. Just how does Chester go about choosing this "ideal" price?

The procedure now is actually not much different from his earlier method of obtaining maximum profits. Therefore, what he is really seeking is the right *output* that will give him the most profits; i.e., he will continue to produce balers so long as the *extra cost* (marginal cost) of producing a baler is lower than the *extra revenue* (marginal revenue) of selling that baler.

Notice our new term "marginal revenue." It can be defined as "the extra revenue gained from selling an extra unit of output." Remember when Chester was a competitive hay supplier? Recall that the marginal revenue was exactly the same as the price of hay; that is, if he sold an extra load of hay, he would always receive an additional amount of revenue equal to the price.

But now, because of the industry's downward sloping demand curve, marginal revenue will be something *different* from the price. To see this point more clearly, it would be helpful to work out an illustration. Our example will also help show us how Chester chooses the "ideal" quantity to maximize profits.

First, let's work out Chester's industry demand curve using an extremely simplified situation. We will say, for example, that if Chester charges $1,000 for a baler, he wouldn't sell any, but at $900, he will sell one. If he drops his price further, say to $800, he'll sell two, $700, three, and so on. Below, in the first two columns, is Chester's "demand schedule."

(Q) Quantity	(P) Price	(TR) Total Revenue	(MR) Marginal Revenue
0	$1,000	$0	--
1	$ 900	$900	$900
2	$ 800	$1600	$700
3	$ 700	$2100	$500
4	$ 600	$2400	$300
5	$ 500	$2500	$100
6	$ 400	$2400	-$100

Next, let's work out the *total revenue*. Chester carefully calculates his total revenue by multiplying price times quantity—and then places these figures in the third column.

From the total revenue column, Chester now can easily calculate what will be his additional revenue from selling an extra unit—i.e., the "marginal revenue." For example, the marginal revenue (MR) of the second unit (#2) is $1600 minus $900 or $700, while the MR of the fifth unit would be $2500 minus $2400 or $100. All the other marginal revenue values were calculated in the same way. Note the interesting relationship between the marginal revenue of a given unit and its price. MR in each case (except for the first unit) is *lower* than P.

Next, by graphing Chester's marginal revenue curve against the demand curve we can actually "see" these relationships (Figure 9-2).

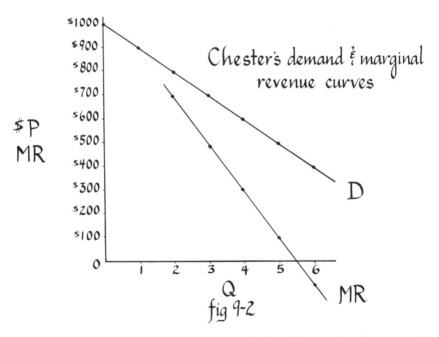

OK so far. Chester now knows what his demand and marginal revenue curves look like. What's next?

In order to make profit maximizing "marginal decisions," Chester must find out what his *marginal costs* are. In that we are also interested in the "efficiency question," we will help him work out his long run average cost curve (LAC) as well. In Figure 9-3, all the relevant curves are drawn on the same graph.

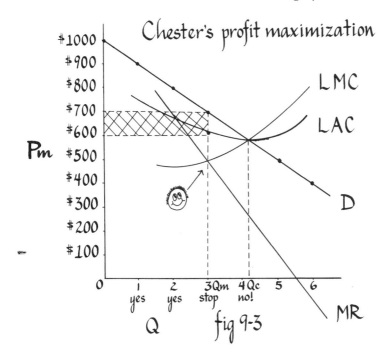

Thus, the above diagram gives Chester all the information he needs to maximize his profits via the old "marginal decision" making approach.

The first question Chester asks himself is, "Is the first unit profitable?" The answer is a resounding "yes" since we can easily see that unit #1 gives Chester far more revenue than it costs him to produce.

His next question is, "How about the second unit?" Again, the answer is "yes." But this time it will be a smaller marginal profit since MR is rapidly dropping. The third unit is obviously the quantity where Chester ought to stop. And past unit three, we see the MR dropping very fast while MC is speedily climbing, and thus no hope exists for any more profitable units.

While this example shows the logic of marginal decision making, there is no reason why we cannot use our "short cut" method where we say that maximum profits are only possible at that quantity *where marginal cost equals marginal revenue.* In other words, we can simply find where the MR and MC curves cross and then "dot" down to the right quantity. From now on we will use this simpler method.

Pricing and Efficiency—

Once we have found out that Chester will maximize his profits at 3 units (Q_m), we can then put our "Sherlock Holmes kits" to work in order to trace all the other relevant information concerning a monopoly operation. All important monopoly results can be "seen" on Figure 9-3. For example,

a. monopoly price—"dot" up from Q_m to the demand curve, then go straight over to the price axis...monopoly price (P_m) in this example is $700 per unit

b. average cost—again "dot" up from Q_m, but this time *stop* at the LAC curve, then go over again to the y axis...average cost is $600

c. per unit profit—if each unit sells for $700, but average cost is $600, Chester makes $100 per unit profit

d. total profit—selling three units, and making $100 per unit, gives Chester a total profit of $300.

Figure 9-3 shows us what the output and price *would have been* in a long run competitive situation. From the last chapter we learned that a competitive market tends to generate a long run price that is equivalent to the lowest possible average cost (lowest point on the LAC curve). Using Figure 9-3, we can also see that the competitive price would have been just under $600. Also the competitive quantity can be found by "dotting" down from the low point on LAC. We find it to be quantity Q_c, or just a little more than 4 units.

Therefore, some advantages of the competitive model over the monopoly system are:

a. competition offers a lower price to the consumer

b. competition forces a larger output that is more in line with the optimum scale of production

Putting it another way, the disadvantage of the monopoly market structure is that monopolists nearly always create an "artificial scarcity" and at the same time, charge a price *higher than its marginal cost*. The net result is a misallocation of the economy's resources.

Monopoly Profits —

What often irritates people about monopoly behavior is that monopolies seem to make an unusually large amount of profits — simply because of the company's considerable control of the market. Indeed, this is the case in our "pretend" example of Chester Olson. We can also see "real life" examples of large monopoly profits, too, such as in the case of the Middle East OPEC oil producers, and in many other examples as well. What might surprise you, however, is the fact that monopolists do not *always* make such excessive profits. Why not?

The reason is that profits are always dependent upon a favorable average cost situation in relation to the demand curve. In other words, it's *possible* that Chester could become so complacent as a businessman that he would allow his average cost curve to creep up above the $700 price. Indeed, if this should happen, monopolist Chester Olson would actually *lose* money. (An unusual situation for sure, but still possible.)

Yet, assuming that Chester does in fact earn a significant monopoly profit, can we then say that these profits are *unjustified*? Some people would probably answer this question in the affirmative. However, there may be some justification to profits such as these, both for monopolists and for other businesses operating under imperfect competitive situations. For example, it is generally acknowledged by economists that some profits are a legitimate return for *innovation*. In Chester's case, one would have a difficult time arguing that Chester did not deserve some financial reward for his superior hay-baling machine. In addition, Chester should probably receive some kind of monetary reward for the financial *risk* that was involved in undertaking this hazardous venture. And finally, economists recognize the suitability of a certain amount of profits for Chester's effective co-ordination of resources — i.e., his *entrepreneurial abilities*.

Still, economists worry that *any* degree of monopoly or of monopolization of a market will ultimately result in a "less efficient" use of society's limited resources — as compared to a more competitive situation. Furthermore, monopoly profits are not always a result of legitimate innovation or risk, but often come about as a result of blocking entry to the industry.

Or, what is perhaps more often the case, monopoly profits are a result of a *trust, cartel, or shared monopoly*. These three terms refer to a situation in which groups of producers get together to carve up markets and fix prices and therefore act *as if* they were one large monopoly. Profits derived from such collusion are definitely considered *unjustified*.

The problems concerning profits and monopoly behavior lead us to the question, "What can be done about it?" Let's take a brief look at some of the methods of dealing with monopoly.

Dealing with Monopoly—

Perhaps the easiest type of monopoly both to recognize and to deal with is the natural monopoly such as a public utility. As we learned earlier, a natural monopoly comes about because of scale requirements. Thus a phone company, for example, can be allowed a "legal status" as a monopolist as long as it consents to be *regulated* by some publically appointed commission. The regulators, in turn, can establish a non-monopoly price and quantity more in line with what would have been the case under competitive conditions.

Another method of eliminating unjustified monopoly profits is simply to "tax them away" by a fixed or *lump-sum tax*. For example, if the government had deemed all of Chester's profits as "unjustified," it could tax him the full $300 profit; this would have the effect of raising his LAC curve by $100, making it a no-profit situation in which the price would equal average cost. The drawback of this "solution" is that it leaves Chester's old MR = MC intact, and thus he will continue to produce at an "artificial scarcity" level of Q_m as he did in the earlier example (see Figure 9-3). Perhaps you are wondering why Chester would want to produce at all if there were no profits involved. The answer to this legitimate query is the same as when Chester was a "competitor." That is, when we draw the cost curves, we are assuming that *all* costs are covered—including a fair rate of return on his investment.

For cartels and predatory monopolies, we have a slightly different situation. For one thing, these monopolies are difficult to recognize—and then once recognized, the government must *legally prove* their anti-competitive behavior. Yet, when monopoly behavior can be proven, it's illegal under our *anti-trust laws*. Firms violating these laws can be penalized with stiff fines, and individual executives responsible for the illegal decisions may even go to jail.

There are also certain types of monopolies that are even more difficult to deal with than those mentioned above. Ivan Illich, in his book *Tools for Conviviality*, identifies what he calls *radical monopolies* which involve the dominance of large product systems:

> I speak about radical monopoly when one industrial production process exercises an exclusive control over the satisfaction of a pressing need...Cars can thus monopolize traffic. They can shape a city into their image—practically ruling out locomotion on foot or by bicycle in Los Angeles.*

Illich has also written about radical monopolies in the form of schooling (*Deschooling Society*) and modern medicine (*Medical Nemesis*)—monopolies, where, in each case, the public has no practical alternative.

If Illich's conclusions are correct, radical monopolies may pose greater problems for an economic system than industrial or corporate monopolies. Indeed, this is one more important area that needs more research from the social sciences.

And surely, the understanding of an economic monopoly can help us understand and deal with it in other guises. For example, a political dictatorship or a one-party state is a form of monopoly, too. One might also look at the parent-child relationship as a monopoly—a theme that is explored in John Holt's book *Escape from Childhood*. I'm sure you can think up your own examples.

Yet, however we look at the monopoly concept—whether in purely economic terms, or in its broader context—it is usually bad news. It involves a *no-alternative situation* for the "consumer." It is a situation where the competitive system of checks and balances are absent allowing the monopolist to magnify and accentuate man's tendency to hurt and exploit others in his pursuit of his own profits and power.

---

*Tools for Conviviality, by Ivan Illich © 1973 Harper & Row, p. 55.

Chapter 10

Oligopoly and Differentiated-Competition

In this, our final chapter, we are going to move one more step closer to reality as we round out our discussion of the imperfectly competitive market structures. More specifically, we're going to take a look at the *oligopoly* and *differentiated-competitive* systems—certainly, the two most prevalent industry structures in the U.S. today.

We will again have the benefit of our earlier production and cost analysis as well as the tools we developed to find maximum profit via the marginal decision approach. Nothing will change in this area. What does change as we shift from one system to another is the relative *control* that any individual firm will have in its specific market. This difference, in turn, gives rise to different *demand curves*. Let's see how this works by first taking up oligopoly.

Oligopoly—

What is an oligopoly? An oligopoly market structure is a market in which the entire industry is *dominated by just a few firms*. In most cases, the single oligopolist markets a product that he considers "different" from his rivals.

In addition, oligopolists try to promote their products not so much by offering the lowest price possible (i.e., by "price competition"), but by a variety of techniques which are lumped under the title *non-price competition*.

Non-price competition includes things like stylistic differences, brand name recognition, advertising, service, quality (real or imagined), special location and so on. This kind of competition can be as honest as a "Five-year Unconditional Warranty" or true craftsmanship-like construction, or as dishonest as linking up the buyer with an improbable image of sexual or financial success. Price cutting, however, is generally frowned upon, as it would have the effect of disrupting the industry as well as destabilizing corporate earnings.

What are examples of oligopoly industries? They are not difficult to name since they're the industries which literally dominate the American economic scene; i.e., chemicals, autos, farm machinery, petroleum, pharmaceuticals, metals, tobacco, T.V. manufacture and broadcasting, food processing...just to name a few examples.

And like monopolies, oligopolies exist because of a variety of *entry barriers,* ranging from scale requirements to an inability to raise capital, to building up a brand name. You might, for example, wish to think through the possible obstacles you would face yourself in attempting to start-up a new automobile company, or market a new breakfast cereal, or manufacture and sell over-the-counter drugs. Besides the problem of large-scale manufacturing requirements, you would also face the problems of *gaining access to* and *getting the confidence of* money lenders, researchers, specialized production experts—on through the stages, up to distributors and ultimately, the consumers themselves. At each stage, you would most likely face great difficulties as you attempted to chisel into the existing industrial edifice, break down rigidities, rearrange traditional industrial patterns, and fend off the skilled guerrilla activity of the dominant producers.

Another important characteristic of oligopoly is what economists call *mutual interdependence* — a concept which can be best explained by making a comparison with the pure competitor. Recall that Chester Olson as a farmer competitor *did not care* what his neighbor farmers were doing. Sure, he might be curious, possibly envious, if Jones across the way bought a new tractor or built a new barn. But what Farmer Jones did (or what any other single competitor did) would not, in any way, affect Olson's economic situation.

In contrast, the oligopolist is extremely concerned about what his fellow industrial rivals are doing in terms of pricing, styling, advertising and so forth. At times, this interdependence becomes as complicated as a chess game, and in some cases, as deadly serious as warfare.*

Interdependence, in turn, makes it very difficult to design an appropriate oligopoly theory that is as predictable as our models for perfect competition and monopoly. A good analogy would be for someone to try to develop a predictable theory for the game strategy of a football game; indeed, it would be possible to make one up that would be accurate some of the time, but not all the time.

And so with oligopoly, we are able to devise theories that work part of the time. One of the theories that is commonly cited is called "oligopoly under a kinked demand curve." Let's see what this particular model says about oligopoly behavior.

Kinked Demand Curve—

Why is there so little "price competition" among oligopolists? Why do these industries tend to display rigid pricing policies? Can we actually *prove* that price inflexibility is consistent with profit maximization? The kinked demand curve will help us answer these questions.

To begin our discussion, let's assume that over the years Chester Olson loses his monopoly position as a manufacturer of hay balers. New baler companies have now moved into the market with a similar product and the old standbys like John Deere, International Harvester, New Holland, etc. re-establish themselves.

Thus, Chester is now one of a half-dozen oligopolists within this particular industry. And since we no longer have a monopoly, we will assume that the overall industrial price for balers is established first by the largest company (say John Deere), i.e., the *price leader*, and then the other firms (including Chester's) follow right along. We will call this established price the *administered price* (P_A).

Given the existence of a general administered price, what might Chester's *demand curve* look like? Apparently, if Chester

---

*For an excellent discussion of these aspects of businesses and businessmen, I highly recommend Michael Maccoby's book, *The Gamesman*. (Bantam, 1976)

raises his price, the rest of the producers will *not* be too greatly concerned. Why? Because the rest of the industry will gladly watch Chester *lose* part of his market share by unilaterally raising his price. Thus, when Chester raises his price, he would, in a sense, be "going it alone," and would find himself losing lots of business. The very fact that he will lose a large market share implies that he is on a fairly *elastic demand curve*. We will call this portion, "Chester's own demand curve." Of course, our friend will think twice about raising his price.

Another strategy would be to *lower* his price in hopes of capturing a larger share of the market for himself. Indeed, this plan could be OK for Chester—as long as the rest of the industry *left him alone*. But, of course, they won't leave him alone, because they are not willing to lose business to the "Olson Baler Company." Thus, if Chester lowers his price, the other sellers will follow right along— forcing Chester to move onto the *industry demand curve*.

The industry demand curve will therefore be much less elastic than Chester's "own" demand curve. Thus, Chester might gain a few more sales from lowering his price, but probably not very many more as all the other producers will be lowering their prices right along with him.

In summary, Chester could stand to lose a lot of sales by raising his price, but if he lowers his price, the rest of the industry will follow suit and Chester's extra sales will be minimal. More specifically, what this means for Chester is that he faces *two distinctly different demand curves*. The demand curve above the administered price will be very elastic, while the one below P_A will be much less elastic. And when these two curves are combined on one diagram, it results in a strange looking overall demand for Chester that has a "kink" in it (see Figure 10-1).

You must already have a "feeling" as to why Chester would be reluctant to make price changes. There is apparently no practical reason to raise his price, and not much to gain by lowering it either. Indeed, one's instincts concerning this price inflexibility can in fact be proved. How? By showing that when prices are left alone, Chester is in a maximum profit position. Let's see how this works.

Profit Maximization—

To find out where Chester attains his greatest profit, we will

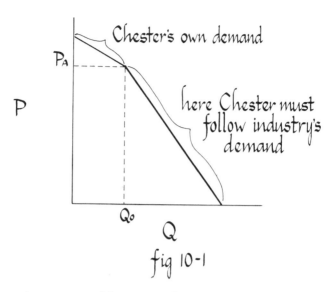

Chester's own demand

P_A

P

here Chester must follow industry's demand

Q_0

Q

fig 10-1

once again use our old system of *marginal decision making*; i.e., profits are maximized only at that quantity where the marginal cost is equal to the marginal revenue (MR = MC). But this process raises a very interesting question, "What will the marginal revenue curve look like in relation to this strange 'kinked' demand curve?"

Actually, the MR curve will look quite similar to the curve as we developed it for the monopolist. This implies that MR will lie somewhere below the demand curve. The only difference is that now we are dealing with two demand curves and will therefore have two MR curves—each falling below their respective demand lines and also reflecting the different demand curve slopes. In reference to Figure 10-1, we can say that up to Q_0, the relevant MR curve is that one associated with the very elastic demand curve, and after Q_0, Chester would be operating on the less elastic "industry" demand curve and would, therefore, have a relatively steep-sloped MR curve. Below in Figure 10-2, we have drawn the two MR curves, and we have also added some sample marginal cost curves in order to help us find Chester's "profitability point."

Note that because the kinked demand curve has two distinct slopes, it causes the two separate MR curves to be *discontinuous*, i.e., there is a long break in the curve directly under the kink and above Q_0. It is, in fact, this discontinuous section that provides us with the major clue to price rigidity in oligopoly markets. Why do we say this?

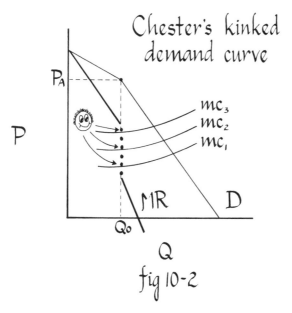

Chester's kinked demand curve

fig 10-2

Because no matter where MC intersects in the vertical discontinuous section of MR, Chester will achieve his maximum profit (MC = MR). In Figure 10-2, we have drawn three different marginal cost curves, MC_1, MC_2, and MC_3; and in each case, we observe the maximum profit point (see Chester smiling?) in the same vertical plane.

Chester then "dots" down to the x axis to find maximum profit Q, and then up to the demand curve and over to the y axis to find maximum profit P. In each case, the "right" quantity turns out to be Q_0 and the "right" price is P_A or the administered price...and thus the tendency for Chester (as well as all the other producers) to stabilize the price in order to gain maximum profits!

We are now approaching the end of our explorations into microeconomics. But there is one more market which I think will interest you. This market model is officially called "monopolistic competition." The term, however, may lead one to think that monopolistic competition is a market that falls near the monopoly end of the spectrum—or perhaps falls evenly between the two extremes of monopoly and competition.

Actually, monopolistic competition is a structure that is *far closer* to the decentralized competitive market. Because of this, we will use a different term that seems to describe the model more accurately—*differentiated-competition*. What then is this new model and how does it relate to the other market structures? Let's now take a look.

Differentiated-Competition —

I almost always enjoy discussing the differentiated-competitive model. Why? I'm not exactly sure, but perhaps it is because the model typifies the small operators—the "little guys"—who strike out on their own in an attempt to become "their own boss." Of course, it is partly a romantic notion that harks back to the old "free-enterprise ideal"—a value that continues to be deeply ingrained in most of us.

Who exactly are these differentiated-competitors? They are the small restaurant and resort owners, the barbers, the beauticians, those who sell used cars or operate repair shops in large cities. They also include others, from the struggling artists, rock bands, and poets, to craft potters and painters and smaller publishers. A seller in this kind of market will usually share their industry with dozens and dozens, perhaps hundreds and hundreds, of other sellers.

Also, these industries share a characteristic with their pure competitive cousins of *easy entry, easy exit.* Thus, scale requirements are usually not an important factor in entering one of these markets. Easy entry also implies that differentiated-competitors face an uphill struggle to achieve anything more than a "normal" profit for the long run (if they are lucky!).

Indeed, it is these little operators who contribute disproportionately to the overall business mortality statistics—such as the chilling fact that three out of five businesses fail in the first two years of operation.

I have discovered that many students dream of getting into business via the differentiated-competitive route—i.e., to become restaurant managers, artists, photographers, fashion merchandisers, and so on. They like the idea of controlling their own lives and the possibilities of the "little guy" taking an entrepreneurial "fling" at the universe—taking with them their entire savings, twelve hour work days . . . and also using their families for extra help.

Perhaps you are wondering, "Why, this market sounds a lot like pure competition; many, many sellers, easy entry and exit, high risk, little long run profits . . . so what is the difference?"

The major difference can be seen in the term "differentiated-competition." That is, each seller has a slightly differentiated product, service, or location. Indeed, there is usually *some difference* between Frank's and Joe's barber shops (or bars), between "Super Sam's Roast Beef" and "The Village Cafeteria," or between the materials, the styles and the quality of the many, many clothing manufacturers. In short, differentiated-competitors have a clearly identifiable product and "brand" name which will attract *some degree* of consumer loyalty.

Consumer loyalty, in turn, means that the seller has a *slight amount* of control over the price. Recall for a minute that a "competitive" seller of corn is a *price taker* who cannot get away with selling his product even a penny above the industry price. In contrast, the "differentiated-competitor" such as a beauty salon, a garage mechanic, or a local bar—usually does have a small amount of price flexibility. Yet, if prices are increased too far "out of line," even the loyal customers will turn away to one of the many alternatives.

Therefore, if we were to draw a differentiated-competitor's demand curve, it would probably be quite *elastic*, but because of product differentiation, it would *not be perfectly elastic*. We have drawn a sample curve in Figure 10-3.

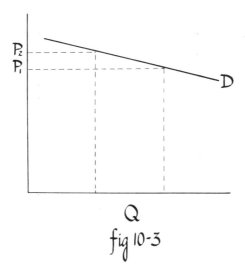

fig 10-3

Note that the differentiated-competitor can raise his price from P₁ to P₂ without losing *all* his customers. A few people will continue to patronize the seller because of the "brand" name or an individualized product or service.

Why don't we once again look up our old friend Chester Olson? Rumor has it that he sold the Olson Baler Company. They say he "bailed out" after he heard that a firm had just developed a revolutionary new baler technology—just as he had done years ago. In the meantime, Chester has let his hair grow long—and he also read a book called *Zen and the Art of Motorcycle Maintenance* which greatly influenced him. So what is he doing now? You guessed it! He is a skilled motorcycle (and bicycle) mechanic in Missoula, Montana. Our friend has now made the rounds—from competition to monopoly to oligopoly; and now he has settled (for good, he says) in a differentiated-competitive market. Since we have already approximated a demand curve for this type of market (Figure 10-3), why don't we simply call this one, "the demand for Chester's motorcycle tune-ups." How then, would Chester maximize his profits this time?

First, he would figure out his marginal revenue curve. As in our earlier example, MR would be a straight line that falls below the very elastic demand curve. Next, Chester computes his long run marginal cost curve, and adds it to the same diagram. In Figure 10-4, we have an approximation of both of these curves.

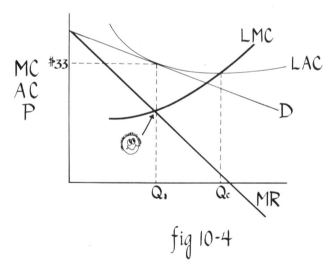

fig 10-4

Where will Chester maximize his profits in Figure 10-4? Like a broken record that keeps repeating its message over and over, "profits are maximized at that quantity where MC = MR." Thus Chester's profit maximizing quantity is Q_1. We then "dot" up to the demand curve to find out what price will be charged. And reading off the y axis, we find that our friend would charge $33 for his comprehensive tune-up.

Next, let's look at the extent of Chester's profits. Our procedure to determine profit is to "dot" up to the LAC curve to find average cost, and then compare this average cost with the price. But upon doing this, Chester is stunned to discover that his average cost *equals* his price—leaving him *no* long run profits. Why not? What characteristic of this market structure denies sellers a long run profit?

The answer to this question is, "easy entry and easy exit." It's the same reason that there were no extra profits for the pure competitive model. But again, keep in mind that a no-excessive profit situation implies that Chester is still earning a fair wage and is receiving a reasonable rate of return on his investment—but just as when our friend was in the hay baling business, there was no way he could keep other "firms" from easily moving into the industry.

For all those who are interested in getting into a market of differentiated-competition, the "easy entry" characteristic ought to raise a red warning flag! One should perhaps "hope for the best, but expect the worst."

Yet, there is another more optimistic side to this model. That is the possibility of creating such a unique product—such as a fantastic restaurant, a service station with unequaled service, an incredibly good cheese, or such popular poems or songs that will reap "quasi-monopoly" profits while living in a market of differentiated competition. But don't count on it! Those who in the long run "make it big" against the competitive odds are few and far between.

Now if this model has some pluses and some minuses from the producers viewpoint, how does it fare in terms of overall economic *efficiency?* To find out the answer to that question, we must look back at Figure 10-4 for a minute. Notice on this graph that Chester's output is *not* the ideal scale output. That ideal output would be represented by the bottom of his LAC curve. Thus the optimum quantity would be Q_c or that quantity that would prevail under purely competitive conditions.

Thus, firms in differentiated-competition will usually build a *less than optimally efficient* plant and will frequently operate that plant at *under capacity*. This conclusion is not surprising when we actually observe workers in gas stations, barber shops, bars and other small businesses spending many of the hours of the day relatively idle. And even when this condition is obvious, or seems obvious, we often notice some "brand new" seller coming onto the scene because of "easy entry" and this new seller dilutes the market even more.

Nor does this type of market offer the consumer the lowest price possible as did pure competition. Yet, due to the highly elastic demand curve, the price will not be too different from the purely competitive price. You can easily verify this point with Figure 10-4.

To sum up, differentiated-competition *tends to have* (in theory) the following long run drawbacks,

—no extra profits for the producer
—chronic underutilization of resources
—a price that is slightly higher than competitive price

But in conclusion let's also remember that this market has some advantages, too. For one thing, this market gives us a *variety of suppliers to choose from* — after all, who would like to have only two or three possible restaurants from which to choose? Particularly in medium and large cities, these little businesses add a considerable amount of interest, variety, and novelty to city living.

The other advantage — the one which we alluded to earlier — is *symbolic*: It stems from the free enterprise dream. Unrealistic? Yes. But still possible.

What we have here is a group of industries that continues to give one the possibility of escaping from hierarchichal existence, from large bureaucratic offices, or from the suffocating boredom of the factory — if that is what one wants to do. It's like a slot within our basically concentrated economic system, where you can organize your own resources, where you can still test your own entrepreneurial strength, and possibly, just possibly, not only survive, but prosper.

Index